# Rising With Grace

## A Warrior's Spiritual Awakening

Karen Pless Gaines

Published by Karen Pless Gaines Toccoa Georgia,
karenplessgaines@outlook.com
Copyright © 2025 Karen Pless Gaines

ISBN: 979-8-9879003-6-9

# DEDICATION

To every woman who has ever felt the weight of societal expectations, the sting of self-doubt, or the whisper of inadequacy—this book is for you. May these pages be a beacon of hope, a source of strength, and a testament to the boundless power of God's grace residing within you. This is a dedication to the unsung heroines of faith, past and present, who have fought the good fight, finished the race, and kept the faith, inspiring generations to come. It is dedicated to those who have paved the way, who have shown courage in the face of adversity, and who continue to rise above limitations to fulfill God's purpose in their lives. To those women who have poured their lives into ministry, often unseen and unacknowledged, know that your dedication is not in vain, your work matters profoundly, and your reward is immeasurable in the eyes of our Heavenly Father. Your stories are woven into the fabric of this book, a tapestry of faith, perseverance, and divine empowerment. To my fellow warriors of faith, may this work strengthen your resolve and ignite the warrior spirit God has placed within each of you. Let us rise together, empowered by His grace, to conquer any challenge, knowing that our victories are His.

# CONTENTS

# PREFACE

For years, I have had the privilege of walking alongside women in their spiritual journeys, witnessing their struggles, celebrating their triumphs, and sharing in their moments of profound joy and heartbreaking sorrow. Through my work in women's ministry, I've encountered countless stories of women wrestling with feelings of inadequacy, struggling to reconcile their faith with societal expectations, and searching for their place within the church and the world. Many felt unseen, unheard, and undervalued—their potential stifled by limiting beliefs and societal pressures. They grappled with the weight of expectations, often internalizing messages that minimized their worth and abilities. This book is born from those experiences, those conversations, and the overwhelming need for a message of empowerment and hope specifically tailored for Christian women. It is a testament to the incredible strength and resilience of women who, despite facing numerous obstacles, continue to rise above adversity, fueled by their unwavering faith in God. It is my sincere prayer that this book will inspire you, encourage you, and challenge you to embrace the warrior spirit that God has placed within you, step into your full potential, and rise with grace, empowered by the love and grace of our Heavenly Father. I invite you to engage with the scriptures and reflections throughout this book and, most importantly, to connect with the unwavering love and empowerment of the divine. Let this be a journey not just of reading, but of discovery, transformation, and profound spiritual awakening.

# INTRODUCTION

In a world that frequently overlooks and underappreciates the remarkable contributions of women, it is essential to shine a light on the profound influence they have had throughout history and continue to make today. **Rising with Grace: A Warrior's Spiritual Awakening** is a compelling and inspiring exploration of the extraordinary strength and spiritual potential that dwells within every woman. This book challenges the often-narrow narratives that have historically marginalized women, both in societal structures and religious contexts, urging us to recognize their vital roles.

Through an examination of timeless scripture, we will embark on a journey to uncover the lives of exceptional women—Deborah, a fierce leader and prophetess who boldly commanded armies; Jael, whose courage turned the tide of battle singlehandedly; Ruth, whose loyalty and tenacity reshaped her destiny; Hannah, who stood in unwavering faith to fulfill a divine promise; Esther, who risked her life to save her people; and Mary, who embraced her pivotal role in the divine plan. These women were not mere spectators in the grand narrative of salvation; they were dynamic architects of history, each embodying qualities of courage, faith, and transformative leadership. Their powerful stories serve as a vivid reminder of the divine power within every woman, inspiring us to break free from the chains of limiting beliefs and boldly pursue our God-given purpose.

This book is more than just a historical or theological examination; it is a passionate call to action. It invites you to acknowledge the extraordinary strength that God has placed within you, encouraging you to rise above self-doubt and societal expectations. Embrace the warrior spirit that enables you to fight valiantly against life's challenges, finish your unique race with perseverance, and keep your faith unwavering amidst adversity. Prepare to embark on a profound journey of self-discovery, spiritual awakening, and empowerment. Through richly woven scriptural insights, heartfelt personal reflections, and practical guidance tailored for everyday life, this book will equip you with essential tools to uncover your unique spiritual gifts. You will learn to navigate life's complexities with grace and resilience, empowering you to ultimately live a life filled with purpose and fulfillment. Get ready to rise with grace, harness your inherent divine strength, and step into the extraordinary warrior role that God has destined for you. Embrace this journey and unlock the transformative power that awaits within you.

# CHAPTER 1

# UNVEILING THE WARRIOR WITHIN

Imagine yourself sitting by a tranquil lake, the warm sun on your face, a gentle breeze whispering through the reeds. The water reflects the sky, a vast expanse of blue mirroring the boundless potential within you. This is a moment of quiet reflection, a space to unveil the warrior within, a warrior not of brute force, but of unwavering faith, quiet strength, and fierce determination. For within each woman, created in God's image, lies an inherent strength often overlooked, underestimated, and even suppressed by societal and religious narratives that perpetuate the myth of female weakness and submissiveness.

This isn't about ignoring the very real challenges women face – the societal pressures, the cultural expectations, the internalized messages that whisper doubts and insecurities. It's about recognizing the powerful counter-narrative woven into the very fabric of creation, a narrative that celebrates the inherent dignity, worth, and strength bestowed upon every woman by her Creator. Genesis 1:27 declares, "So God created mankind in his own image, in the image of God he created them; male and female he created them." This verse is not about sameness; it's about equality. We are created in the image of a God who is omnipotent, omniscient, and omnipresent – attributes that reflect power, wisdom, and unwavering presence. This inherent image carries with it an inherent strength.

The societal and religious narratives that often diminish female potential are rooted in centuries of misinterpretations and patriarchal structures. The idea of women as inherently weaker, less capable, or secondary to men is a distortion of God's original intent. Throughout history, women have been relegated to roles that undervalue their contributions and suppress their voices. Yet, the Bible is replete with examples of women who shattered expectations, defied norms, and demonstrated extraordinary courage, faith, and leadership. Deborah, a judge in Israel; Jael, who courageously killed Sisera; Esther, who risked her life to save her people; Ruth, whose loyalty and faithfulness are legendary; Hannah, whose persistent prayers were answered; and Mary, whose humble obedience changed the course of history – these are but a few examples of women who embodied the very strength we are exploring. Their stories are not merely historical anecdotes; they are powerful testimonies to the inherent strength residing within each woman.

The strength we're talking about isn't solely physical prowess. It's not about dominating or overpowering others. It's a spiritual strength, a resilience born from a deep and abiding relationship with God. It's the fortitude to face adversity, the courage to stand up for what's right, the determination to pursue your God-given purpose, and the unwavering faith to trust in His plan even when the path ahead is unclear. This strength is not something we earn; it is a gift, a divine endowment, readily available to each of us through faith in Christ.

Consider the image of the lake again. The surface may appear calm, but beneath lies a depth, a power, a force that can be both gentle and overwhelming. Similarly, a woman's outward appearance might suggest fragility or submissiveness, but within dwells a wellspring of strength waiting to be tapped. This strength is not about proving anything to anyone; it's about recognizing the inherent value God placed in you and embracing the potential He has placed within your heart.

This journey of self-discovery is not about self-reliance but about recognizing our dependence on God. Our strength comes not from within ourselves but from the power of God dwelling within us. We are empowered, strengthened, and sustained by His grace. It is through this divine partnership that we can overcome obstacles, navigate challenges, and fulfill our God-given purposes. The warrior within is not a solitary figure battling alone; she is a woman walking in step with her Creator, drawing strength from His unwavering love and guidance.

Think about the women in your life – mothers, sisters, friends, mentors – who have demonstrated remarkable strength in the face of hardship. Their stories, often untold, are testaments to the enduring power of the human spirit, fueled by faith and empowered by God. Their lives reflect the same inherent strength that resides in you.

Let's explore some practical ways to recognize and cultivate this inherent strength:

**Spend time in prayer and meditation:** This allows you to connect with God on a deeper level, receiving His guidance and strength. It's in these moments of quiet communion that we tap into the wellspring of divine power within us. Consider creating a regular practice of prayer and meditation, even if it's just for a few minutes each day. Allow yourself to be still and listen for God's voice.

**Study Scripture:** The Bible is filled with stories of women who overcame tremendous obstacles through their faith. By studying their lives and learning from their experiences, we gain strength and inspiration for our own journeys. Focus on the lives of women like Deborah, Esther, and Ruth. Consider what challenges they faced, how they responded, and the lessons they offer for your life.

**Engage in spiritual disciplines:** Activities such as fasting, journaling, and serving others can deepen your connection with God and help you develop spiritual resilience. Consider incorporating one or two new spiritual disciplines into your routine and see how it impacts your life.

**Build a supportive community:** It is crucial to surround yourself with other Christian women who offer encouragement and support. This community can provide a safe space to share your struggles, celebrate your victories, and receive prayer and encouragement. Join a Bible study group, connect with women in your church, or find an online community of Christian women.

**Identify and challenge limiting beliefs:** Examine the beliefs you hold about yourself and your abilities. Are there any limiting beliefs that are holding you back? Ask God to help you identify and challenge those beliefs, replacing them with truths from His Word. Write down the limiting beliefs and then write a corresponding truth from scripture.

**Embrace your unique gifts and talents:** God has given each of us unique gifts and talents to use for His glory. Take time to identify your strengths and find ways to use them in service to others. Consider volunteering your skills and talents within your church or community.

**Practice self-compassion:** Be kind to yourself, recognizing that you are not perfect and that you will make mistakes. God's love and grace are always available, regardless of your failures. Forgive yourself, learn from your mistakes, and move forward with renewed strength.

The journey to unveiling the warrior within is a lifelong process. It's a journey of self-discovery, spiritual growth, and unwavering faith in a God who has empowered you with an inherent strength beyond measure. It's a journey of embracing your identity as a daughter of the King, a woman created in His image, and a warrior called to live a life of purpose, passion, and unwavering faith. As you continue to walk with the Lord, you will discover depths of strength and resilience that you never knew existed, strength that will empower you to overcome any obstacle and to fulfill the amazing plan God has for your life. The tranquil lake by which you sit is a reminder of the peace and strength you can find in Him, and this peace fuels the fire of your inner warrior.

Many of us carry within us a collection of limiting beliefs— Insidious whispers that chip away at our self-esteem and hinder our ability to embrace the warrior spirit within. These beliefs, often ingrained from childhood, societal pressures, and even well-meaning yet misguided religious interpretations, act as invisible chains, preventing us from stepping into our full potential as daughters of the King. They tell us we're not strong enough, smart enough, capable enough – or worthy enough – to pursue the extraordinary life God intends for us.

These limiting beliefs are not always obvious. They often operate subtly, manifesting as self-doubt, fear of failure, or a persistent sense of inadequacy. They can present themselves as a nagging voice, constantly reminding us of our shortcomings and minimizing our accomplishments. For instance, one woman might believe she's not qualified to lead a ministry despite having the skills and passion for it. Another might feel unworthy to speak out against injustice, despite a burning desire to champion those who are marginalized. A third might suppress her creative talents, fearing judgment or believing her work isn't "good enough." These are all examples of limiting beliefs in action – silent saboteurs hindering God's purpose in a woman's life.

Where do these beliefs originate? They are often a complex blend of internalized messages and external pressures. Societal expectations that dictate women's roles and limit their aspirations play a significant role. The media often perpetuates unrealistic standards of beauty and success, leaving women feeling inadequate and pressured to conform. Cultural norms can pressure women to prioritize others' needs above their own, leading to feelings of self-sacrifice and resentment, further fueling a sense of inadequacy. Even within religious contexts, misinterpretations of scripture can inadvertently reinforce limiting beliefs, portraying women as passive, subservient, or less capable than men.

The insidious nature of these limiting beliefs lies in their ability to disguise themselves as truth. They sound reasonable—almost logical at times—and can be difficult to identify as the source of our self-doubt. For example, the belief "I'm not smart enough to lead a Bible study" might sound logical if a woman lacks a formal theological education. However, the truth is, God can use anyone— regardless of educational background—to be a powerful instrument of His love and truth. The limiting belief masks a deeper spiritual truth: that God equips those He calls, and His power works through our weaknesses.

Overcoming these limiting beliefs requires a conscious and intentional effort. It begins with recognizing their existence. This is often the most challenging step, as we tend to be more aware of our shortcomings than our strengths. It requires a deep introspective process, a willingness to examine our thoughts and feelings honestly, and a willingness to confront the root causes of our self-doubt. Journaling can be invaluable in this process, allowing us to explore our innermost thoughts and feelings without judgment.

Once we've identified these limiting beliefs, the next step is to actively challenge them. This involves replacing negative thoughts with positive affirmations based on God's Word. For example, if we believe "I'm not good enough," we can counter that with scriptures that declare God's unconditional love and acceptance. Verses like Ephesians 1:4-5 – "For he chose us in him before the creation of the world to be holy and blameless in his sight. In love he predestined us for adoption to sonship through Jesus Christ, in accordance with his pleasure and will" – remind us of our inherent worth in Christ.

This process often requires seeking support and accountability. Surrounding ourselves with a community of Christian women who can offer encouragement, affirmation, and prayer can provide the strength we need to break free from these chains. A strong support network can create a safe space to express vulnerability and share struggles without judgment, encouraging each other to step outside their comfort zones and into God's purpose for their lives.

Furthermore, we must embrace the power of God's grace. We are not called to overcome these limitations in our own strength, but through the empowering presence of Jesus Christ. Prayer, fasting, and studying scripture are crucial spiritual disciplines that connect us to the source of all strength and empower us to confront our deepest fears and insecurities. Regular prayer enables us to cast these limiting beliefs onto God, receiving in return His strength, courage, and wisdom to challenge and overcome them. Fasting strengthens our spiritual focus, providing the clarity needed to discern the truth from the lies whispered by these limiting beliefs. Studying scripture provides a solid foundation of truth, and we need to replace the lies with God's promises.

The journey of breaking free from limiting beliefs is not a sprint, but a marathon. It requires patience, persistence, and unwavering faith. There will be setbacks and moments of doubt, but by continuously challenging these limiting beliefs and focusing on

God's truth, we can gradually dismantle these internal obstacles, replacing them with the confidence and assurance of His love and acceptance. As we actively choose to believe in the divine strength He provides, we will progressively unveil the warrior within, stepping into our full potential and fulfilling the remarkable purpose God has placed in our hearts.

Remember the powerful women of scripture: Deborah, a judge who led Israel to victory; Esther, who risked her life to save her people; Ruth, whose loyalty and faithfulness are legendary. Each faced her own unique challenges and overcame them through unwavering faith in God. Their stories serve as potent reminders that the warrior spirit dwells within each of us, waiting to be awakened.

The process of unveiling the warrior within involves identifying specific areas where limiting beliefs might hold us back. For example, perhaps we fear public speaking, which hinders us from sharing our faith or leading in ministry. Or we might hesitate to pursue educational or career goals due to self-doubt about our abilities. Each of these represents a battleground where we can actively choose to challenge the limiting beliefs and replace them with faith-filled affirmations. This could involve stepping outside our comfort zones and embracing new opportunities, even if they initially feel daunting.

The key is to replace the whispers of doubt with the unwavering truth of God's word. Instead of accepting the belief, "I'm too shy to share my faith," we could replace it with the understanding that God empowers us and uses our unique gifts to serve Him. Through prayer, He provides the courage and words we need to share the gospel with others. The same principle applies to any area where limiting beliefs hold sway. We actively replace fear, self-doubt, and feelings of inadequacy with the empowering truth of God's love and unfailing support.

The unveiling of the warrior within is not merely a personal transformation; it's a spiritual awakening. It's about recognizing our inherent worth in God's eyes, embracing our unique gifts, and stepping into His magnificent plan for our lives. It's a journey of continuous growth and spiritual maturity, empowered by the Spirit of God and fueled by the unwavering conviction that we are indeed powerful warriors, daughters of the King, called to make a significant impact on the world. This journey is not about self-reliance or perfection but about relying completely on the empowering grace of God, using the strength and gifts He has given us to walk in His purpose. The warrior within is not a persona to be adopted, but an essence to be unveiled, a strength to be revealed as we abide in Him and walk hand-in-hand with our Lord.

**Extraordinary Women of the Bible**

The journey to unveiling the warrior within is not a solitary trek across a barren landscape; it's a pilgrimage undertaken in the comforting embrace of God's unwavering grace. This grace isn't a mere afterthought, a consolation prize awarded after strenuous self-effort; it's the very bedrock upon which our strength is built, the wellspring from which our courage flows. It's recognizing that our power isn't self-generated but divinely bestowed, a gift freely given, not earned through merit or achievement. This understanding liberates us from the crippling burden of self-reliance, freeing us to embrace our vulnerabilities and find strength in our dependence on God.

Think of the women of scripture, their lives etched in the annals of faith as testaments to the transformative power of God's grace. Deborah, the courageous judge who led Israel to victory, wasn't empowered by her own military prowess, but by the Spirit of God working through her. Her strength stemmed not from a self-assuredness born of her own abilities, but from an unwavering faith in divine guidance and provision. The battle was His; the victory was His; her role was to be His instrument, trusting implicitly in His grace to lead her and empower her every step of the way. It was not about her inherent strength, but the grace that flowed through her.

Similarly, consider Esther, who risked her life to save her people. Her courage wasn't born of a fearless disposition but from a deep-seated trust in God's plan, a reliance on His unseen hand guiding her actions. She was a young woman thrust into an incredibly dangerous situation, yet she acted with boldness, driven not by arrogance or a sense of self-sufficiency, but by a faith fueled by God's grace. Her story is not about a naturally courageous woman but one extraordinarily empowered by a grace that transcended her human limitations. The courage she displayed wasn't her own but was a reflection of God's grace working through her.

Ruth exemplifies this principle even further with her unwavering loyalty and faithfulness. Her life, marked by loss and hardship, reveals the enduring strength found in unwavering reliance on God's goodness and mercy. Her journey was one of profound loss, yet through her dedication to Naomi and her trust in God's grace, she found redemption and unexpected blessing. Her story teaches us the power of faithfulness not as a product of inherent strength but as a testament to God's grace operating in the midst of adversity. It wasn't self-reliance, but a divinely orchestrated grace that sustained her journey.

These women, and many others in scripture, weren't paragons of perfection, devoid of fear or doubt. They were ordinary women who encountered extraordinary circumstances and responded with extraordinary faith, empowered by the extraordinary grace of God. Their stories remind us that our strength isn't contingent upon our personal abilities or accomplishments, but rather on our connection to the divine source of all power.

The grace of God isn't a magic wand that instantly erases all challenges. It doesn't shield us from hardship or pain—but it provides the strength, resilience, and unwavering hope to navigate life's storms. It equips us with the spiritual resources we need to endure, to overcome, and to find unexpected joy and peace even amidst suffering. It's the gentle hand that steadies us when we stumble, the quiet voice that whispers encouragement when we falter, and the powerful presence that sustains us when we feel overwhelmed.

God's grace is not merely a passive force—It actively works within us, shaping our character, refining our faith, and empowering us to become more like Christ. It's the catalyst for transformation, the driving force behind spiritual growth, and the unwavering support that enables us to face any challenge with courage and confidence. It's not about earning God's favor through flawless performance— but about receiving His love and acceptance unconditionally.

Understanding God's grace is crucial in our journey to unveil the warrior within. It's a journey of relinquishing our need for self-reliance and embracing God's empowering presence. It's about acknowledging our weaknesses, limitations, and dependence on God and finding strength and empowerment in that very dependence. It's about recognizing that our inherent worth is not determined by our accomplishments or our perceived inadequacies but by our identity as beloved daughters of the King.

Consider Hannah, whose unwavering faith in God's promise amidst years of barrenness, is a profound example of the power of grace. Her persistent prayer, her unwavering hope, wasn't fueled by self-determination, but by a deep trust in God's timing and His sovereign plan. Her story highlights that God's grace is not limited by our circumstances, but extends its reach into the deepest recesses of our hearts, offering comfort, hope, and strength in times of adversity. It reminds us that God's grace is not dependent on our merits but is freely available to all who seek it.

The transformative power of God's grace isn't confined to biblical times; it's as relevant and transformative today as it ever was. In the midst of our daily struggles, personal challenges, and societal pressures that seek to diminish us, God's grace offers a lifeline, a source of strength, and a pathway to freedom. It empowers us to overcome limiting beliefs, resist negative self-talk, and step confidently into our God-given purpose.

This grace doesn't negate our responsibility to strive for excellence or to work diligently toward our goals. It doesn't excuse laziness or inaction. Rather, it empowers us to do so with a heart free from the crippling burden of self-reliance, confident in the knowledge that our efforts are empowered by a divine force far greater than ourselves.

The process of unveiling the warrior within is not about becoming superhuman, but about becoming fully human, empowered by the grace of God. It's about living authentically, embracing our vulnerabilities, and finding strength in our connection with our Creator. It's about recognizing that true strength isn't about self-sufficiency but about selflessness, a willingness to surrender our own will to the will of God, trusting in His plan for our lives, and allowing His grace to shape us into the women He intended us to be.

Therefore, as we continue on this journey, let us not forget the constant, unwavering support of God's grace. Let it be our guiding light, our source of strength, and the foundation upon which we build our lives as warriors of faith—empowered to make a difference in this world. Let us embrace the power of His grace, not as a means to overcome challenges in our own strength, but as the very essence of our strength, the wellspring of our courage, and the cornerstone of our faith. Let us stand firm, knowing that we are not alone—but surrounded by the love and unwavering support of a gracious God, who empowers us to be all that He created us to be. This empowering grace, this divine strength, will continue to unveil the warrior within each of us, one step at a time.

Deborah, a prophetess and judge in ancient Israel, stands as a towering figure of female leadership in the Old Testament. Her story, recounted in Judges chapters 4 and 5, isn't simply a tale of military triumph; it's a profound illustration of God's empowerment working through a woman to deliver His people. Deborah wasn't a trained warrior; she possessed no inherent military skill. Yet, God chose her to lead Israel against the Canaanite king Jabin and his formidable general, Sisera. Her leadership wasn't based on brute force or political maneuvering, but on spiritual authority and unwavering faith in God's plan. She summoned Barak, a military leader, to join her, but only after receiving God's clear directive to do so. This act underscores the importance of divine guidance and the necessity of listening to God's voice before embarking on any significant endeavor. Deborah's courage lay not in her physical strength, but in her willingness to obey God's command, even when it meant facing seemingly insurmountable odds. The battle against Sisera, depicted vividly in Judges 5, wasn't just a military victory; it was a spiritual one, demonstrating the power of faith in the face of overwhelming opposition. Deborah's Song of Victory, a poetic masterpiece interwoven with faith and praise, cemented her legacy as a woman of profound courage and unwavering faith in God's deliverance. Her actions challenged the patriarchal norms of her time, demonstrating that God's favor and empowerment extend beyond societal expectations.

The story of Jael, also found in Judges 4 and 5, complements Deborah's narrative, providing a compelling example of unexpected heroism. Jael, a wife of Heber the Kenite, is not presented as a warrior, but as a seemingly ordinary woman with extraordinary courage. When Sisera, fleeing defeat at the hands of Barak's army, sought refuge in her tent, Jael acted decisively, killing him with a tent peg. This act, though brutal, was a vital turning point in the war and a crucial element in Israel's victory. Jael's actions were not only brave but also cunning and strategically significant. It was an act of faith and allegiance to God, demonstrating that strength can manifest in many unexpected ways. Her actions were not celebrated for their violence—but for her bravery and faith in God during an extremely high-pressure moment in Israel's battle for freedom. By choosing to side with the oppressed and against the oppressor, Jael revealed a strength of character that resonated through the ages. Her story challenges the notion that women's strength must always be expressed through traditional avenues of leadership. Instead, it shows that strength can take many forms, and that even seemingly inconspicuous actions can have profound consequences when fueled by faith and courage.

Esther, the heroine of the book named after her, presents another compelling example of feminine strength exercised in a royal court. Her story—one of courage, cunning, and divine providence, showcases a different facet of female leadership. Esther, an orphaned Jewish woman, found herself elevated to the position of queen in the Persian empire, a position that afforded her significant influence—but also considerable risk. Her people, the Jews, faced annihilation at the hands of Haman, the king's wicked advisor. Esther, warned by her cousin Mordecai, was faced with an impossible choice: to remain silent and allow her people to be slaughtered or to risk her own life by confronting the king, an action punishable by death. Choosing faith over fear, she bravely approached the king, unveiling the plot against her people and exposing Haman's treachery. This act of incredible courage was not impulsive but the result of prayer, fasting, and trust in God's plan. Esther's story underscores the importance of using one's position, however obtained, for the benefit of others. It shows that true strength lies not in dominance or aggression—but in selfless service and a willingness to put one's life on the line for a cause greater than oneself. Her actions were not driven by a desire for power—but by a deep love for her people and a profound faith in God's ability to deliver them.

These are just three examples among many. Hannah, the mother of Samuel, exemplifies unwavering faith in the face of prolonged barrenness, a significant societal stigma in her time. Her persistent prayer and unwavering trust in God's promise demonstrate a quiet strength that ultimately led to a profound blessing. Ruth, a Moabite woman, demonstrated unwavering loyalty and faithfulness to her mother-in-law Naomi, highlighting the strength found in compassion, commitment, and steadfastness. Her devotion and perseverance brought her unexpected blessings, showcasing the power of love and dedication. Even Mary, the mother of Jesus, displays immense courage and faith in accepting her role in God's plan, despite the immense social and personal challenges. Her willingness to trust God's call and to bear the burden of bringing the Messiah into the world testifies to the immense faith that resided within her.

The common thread that links these diverse women—Deborah, Jael, Esther, Hannah, Ruth, and Mary—is their unwavering faith and reliance on God. Their actions weren't fueled by self-reliance or a desire for personal glory, but by a deep-seated trust in God's power and His ability to work through them. They faced daunting challenges, societal pressures, and personal fears, but they persevered, guided by their faith and empowered by God. Their stories serve as inspiring examples for women today, demonstrating that God's grace and empowerment are not limited by gender, culture, or circumstance. The women in the Bible display a wide range of leadership styles and expressions of faith, demonstrating that God calls women into various roles and equips them with the necessary strength for each unique task. These biblical narratives illustrate that strength isn't solely about physical power or dominance but is comprised of faith, courage, perseverance, compassion, and a willingness to surrender to God's will.

These biblical accounts provide a rich tapestry of feminine strength, defying simplistic definitions and challenging societal norms. Each woman's journey is unique, yet they collectively demonstrate that God's power is made manifest through vulnerable, faithful women who trust in His guidance and act in accordance with His will. They demonstrate that true strength stems not from self-sufficiency, but from reliance on a divine power that empowers and sustains them. Their stories offer a blueprint for modern women of faith, reminding us that we, too, can be warriors of faith, drawing strength from the same wellspring of grace that empowered these extraordinary women of scripture. Their legacies echo through time, inspiring future generations to discover and embrace the warrior within, empowered by the grace of God. By studying these examples, we not only understand the historical context of these women—but also gain invaluable insight into the enduring power of faith and the potential for divine empowerment that resides within each of us. It's a strength that is not self-generated, but a gift freely given and nurtured through unwavering faith and trust in God's sovereign plan.

The significance of studying these women extends beyond mere historical analysis. Their stories offer practical, applicable lessons for women today. Deborah's leadership teaches the importance of seeking divine guidance before embarking on any significant endeavor, highlighting that leadership stems from faith and a commitment to God's will. Jael's courage shows that strength can be expressed in unexpected ways, often through seemingly small acts of faith and defiance against injustice. Esther's story underscores the necessity of using influence and power for good, demonstrating how courage and faith can make a profound difference even in seemingly insurmountable circumstances. Hannah's story encourages perseverance in prayer, while Ruth's illustrates the importance of loyalty and steadfastness in relationships. Mary's example emphasizes the significance of humble obedience to God's call, even when it requires immense sacrifice.

Understanding these women within their historical and cultural contexts adds further depth to their stories. The societal norms and expectations placed upon women in ancient Israel and Persia differed significantly from those of today. Yet, these women consistently rose above those expectations, demonstrating a strength of character that transcended their cultural limitations. Studying their context allows for a richer understanding of the challenges they overcame and the faith that sustained them. By analyzing their struggles and triumphs, we learn to appreciate the resilience of the human spirit and the transformative power of faith in the face of adversity. Their lives weren't idyllic; they faced hardship, loss, and opposition. Yet, through it all, they demonstrated an unwavering faith that empowered them to overcome obstacles and achieve extraordinary things.

Moreover, analyzing these examples helps us identify the different facets of strength that God empowers within women. These stories demonstrate that strength isn't monolithic; it manifests in diverse ways, shaped by individual personalities, circumstances, and God's unique calling. Some women demonstrate strength through decisive leadership, others through quiet acts of faith and service, and still others through unwavering loyalty and perseverance. Understanding these diverse expressions of strength broadens our own understanding of what it means to be a strong woman of faith, allowing us to appreciate the many ways God uses His power to shape and empower his daughters. It challenges us to move beyond limited, stereotypical notions of strength and to embrace the unique potential and talents that God has gifted each woman.

In conclusion, the biblical accounts of these courageous women serve as both historical narratives and timeless examples of feminine strength empowered by God. When studied carefully and prayerfully, their stories offer invaluable insights into faith, courage, leadership, and the transformative power of God's grace. These women were not perfect; they were flawed, yet faithful, demonstrating that God works powerfully through imperfect vessels. Their lives are not simply historical records, but living testaments to the transformative power of God's grace and a powerful reminder to every woman reading that the warrior within is waiting to be unveiled, empowered by the same divine force that guided these remarkable women of faith. They serve as enduring reminders that every woman possesses within her the potential for strength, resilience, and unwavering faith—a strength that is not self-generated, but a gift freely given by a loving and powerful God.

Embracing your God-given purpose is not a passive endeavor; it's an active pursuit, a journey of discovery guided by prayer, introspection, and a willingness to listen to the gentle nudges of God. It's about aligning your passions, talents, and values with God's will, allowing Him to shape your unique path and empower you to fulfill your divinely ordained destiny. This isn't about striving for worldly success or recognition—but about aligning your life with God's purpose for your life, a purpose far greater and more fulfilling than any earthly ambition.

The first step in this journey is introspection – taking the time to examine your gifts, passions, and values. What are you naturally drawn to? What activities bring you joy and fulfillment? What causes stir your heart and inspire you to act? Often, our passions are clues to our purpose. God has uniquely gifted each of us, bestowing talents and abilities designed to serve His kingdom and bless others. These gifts may be obvious—a talent for teaching, music, writing, or leadership—or they may be more subtle, a capacity for empathy, compassion, or unwavering support. Identifying these gifts is crucial; they are the building blocks of your unique contribution to God's grand design.

Consider keeping a journal specifically for this purpose. Record your thoughts, feelings, and experiences. Note instances where you felt particularly alive, engaged, and fulfilled. Reflect on moments when you felt a strong sense of purpose or calling. Pray for discernment and guidance. Ask God to reveal your unique gifts and how He desires to use them to further His kingdom. Don't be afraid to explore different avenues, to try new things, and to step outside your comfort zone. God often works in mysterious ways, leading us down paths we never anticipated and revealing His purpose for us in unexpected circumstances.

Spiritual disciplines are essential in this process. Regular prayer, Bible study, and fellowship with other believers will provide the spiritual nourishment and guidance you need. Through prayer, you open your heart to God's guidance, inviting Him to illuminate your path and empower you to follow His will. Through Bible study, you gain a deeper understanding of God's character, His promises, and His plan for your life. And through fellowship with other believers, you find support, encouragement, and accountability as you navigate this journey. Remember, you are not alone; God has placed a community of believers around you to support and encourage you.

Discernment is a key element in identifying your God-given purpose. It's the ability to recognize God's voice amidst the noise and distractions of daily life. It involves careful consideration of your circumstances, opportunities, and the needs of those around you. God often speaks through circumstances, opening doors or closing others, presenting opportunities and challenges that shape our path. He speaks through Scripture, providing guidance and wisdom that illuminate our choices and decisions. He may speak through the counsel of trusted mentors or spiritual advisors, providing encouragement and support as we journey toward our purpose.

Developing a plan is crucial once you have a sense of your purpose. A plan provides structure, focus, and a sense of direction. It's not a rigid, inflexible roadmap; instead, it's a flexible guideline that can be adjusted and refined as you gain clarity and experience. Consider setting short-term and long-term goals, breaking down larger objectives into smaller, manageable steps. Pray regularly as you develop this plan, seeking God's guidance and wisdom. Consider what resources you will need—time, finances, support—and seek ways to acquire them. Remember that developing a plan requires both faith and action. It is an expression of your trust in God's plan for your life and a demonstration of your willingness to participate actively in the fulfillment of His purpose.

Overcoming obstacles is an inevitable part of pursuing your God-given purpose. Challenges and setbacks are opportunities for growth and refinement. They test our faith, strengthen our resolve, and deepen our dependence on God. During these times, remember to rely on prayer, seeking God's strength and guidance. Surround yourself with supportive individuals who can offer encouragement, accountability, and practical assistance. Remember God's promises, drawing strength and hope from His Word. Understand that setbacks are not necessarily failures; they are learning experiences, refining your abilities, and shaping your character. View these challenges as opportunities for growth, strengthening your faith, and deepening your reliance on God's grace.

Celebrating your successes is equally important. As you achieve milestones along your journey, take time to acknowledge and appreciate God's blessings. Express gratitude for His guidance, His provision, and His empowering presence. Celebrate your victories, sharing them with those who have supported you. This will encourage you, and those around you, to continue on your path of purpose. This affirmation fuels continued growth and inspires others to embrace their own God-given potential. Celebrating success is not about self-congratulation, but about recognizing God's hand in your life and expressing gratitude for His abundant blessings.

Remember, the journey of embracing your God-given purpose is a lifelong process. It is a journey of growth, learning, and deepening faith. It involves continuous refinement, adjustment, and trust in God's guidance. As you embark on this journey, embrace the challenges, celebrate the victories, and trust in God's unwavering support. Your purpose is not a destination to be reached, but a path to be followed, constantly evolving and deepening as you grow in your relationship with God. It's about living a life that honors Him, blesses others, and fulfills your unique potential as a daughter of the King. This is not simply a career or vocation, but a lifestyle rooted in faith, service, and a deep commitment to God's will.

Furthermore, the pursuit of your God-given purpose is not a solitary endeavor. It's a journey undertaken in community, surrounded by fellow believers who offer support, encouragement, and accountability. Engage in fellowship with other Christians, sharing your struggles and triumphs, seeking wisdom and guidance from those who have walked a similar path. Be involved in your church community, serving others and using your gifts to contribute to the growth and well-being of the body of Christ. This communal aspect enhances your journey, providing both emotional and practical support as you navigate the challenges and celebrate the victories of living a purposeful life.

Finally, remember that your God-given purpose is not a static concept; it can evolve and change over time. As you grow in your faith and experience, your understanding of your purpose may deepen and your path may shift. Be open to God's guidance, allowing Him to lead you in new directions and equip you with new skills and opportunities. Embrace flexibility, trusting in His plan for your life and his ability to adapt it as you go. This flexibility ensures that your purpose remains relevant and aligned with God's will, always leading you to fulfillment and spiritual growth. The beauty of this journey is the ongoing unfolding of God's plan, a continuous revelation that strengthens your faith and deepens your relationship with your creator. The journey of discovering and fulfilling your God-given purpose is not a race, but a marathon of faith, perseverance, and unwavering trust in the divine guidance of God's will in your life.

## Discussion Questions

1. How does the imagery of the tranquil lake relate to the concept of inner strength and potential within each woman?

2. In what ways have societal and religious narratives distorted the perception of women's strength throughout history?

3. Can you identify any personal experiences where you felt the "warrior within" emerge? What triggered that strength?

4. Why is it important to recognize the inherent dignity and worth bestowed upon women, as highlighted in Genesis 1:27?

5. How do the stories of women like Deborah, Esther, and Ruth inspire you in your own life?

6. What does spiritual strength mean to you, and how can it differ from physical or societal notions of strength?

7. How can prayer and meditation help in cultivating a deeper connection with God and recognizing your own strengths?

8. Reflect on the influential women in your life. What qualities or strengths have they demonstrated that resonate with the themes discussed?

9. In what practical ways can you regularly engage with Scripture to draw inspiration and strength from the examples of women in the Bible?

10. How can community support and shared experiences enhance our recognition of strength among women?

# CHAPTER 2

# DEBORAH: LEADERSHIP AND COURAGE

Deborah's story, etched in the pages of Judges 4 and 5, stands as a powerful testament to a woman's unwavering faith and courageous leadership in the face of overwhelming adversity. It's a narrative that resonates deeply with women today, challenging societal norms and religious interpretations that often diminish the significant roles women have played throughout history and continue to play in God's kingdom. Her life wasn't defined by passivity or acceptance of oppression; instead, she actively engaged with God's calling, demonstrating remarkable strength, strategic acumen, and a profound trust in divine guidance.

The backdrop of Deborah's life was one of deep-seated oppression. The Israelites, God's chosen people, were subjugated under the tyrannical rule of Jabin, King of Canaan, whose army, commanded by the ruthless Sisera, terrorized the land for twenty years. This prolonged period of oppression, characterized by fear, insecurity, and the constant threat of violence, created an atmosphere of despair and hopelessness. Yet, amidst this darkness, Deborah emerged as a beacon of hope and defiance. She wasn't merely a prophetess; she was a judge, a leader, a military strategist, and a woman of unwavering faith. This multifaceted role underscores the multifaceted nature of God's calling upon women, a calling that transcends societal expectations and embraces a wide spectrum of talents and abilities.

The Bible portrays Deborah as a woman who sat under the palm tree of Deborah, dispensing justice and offering spiritual guidance to her people. This imagery speaks volumes about her accessibility and the trust she inspired. People came to her not only for legal counsel but also for spiritual direction and encouragement. Her presence was a source of strength and hope in a time of profound darkness. The fact that she judged Israel underscores her authority and the recognition she received from God and His people. This wasn't a position of power she sought or claimed; it was a role bestowed upon her by divine appointment, a testament to God's willingness to use women in leadership positions.

Deborah's role as a judge wasn't simply about resolving disputes. In a patriarchal society, where women often lacked significant influence, her ability to administer justice demonstrates a powerful rejection of societal norms and limitations. It was a courageous act of defiance, a visible declaration that God's justice extended beyond gender boundaries and that women could and should participate fully in administering His justice. Her actions shattered the conventional expectations of a woman's role in society, opening pathways for future generations of women to challenge oppressive systems and champion the cause of justice.

Her prophetic call to Barak, a courageous but hesitant military leader, is a pivotal moment in her narrative. She didn't shy away from confronting his doubts and challenging him to step into his God-given role. Her message was clear: God had commanded victory, and Barak's responsibility was to lead the army. Her words are a powerful reflection of the role women play in empowering others, encouraging them to embrace their potential and step forward in faith. Deborah's guidance was not simply directive; it was infused with the wisdom and strength that came from an intimate relationship with God.

This wasn't a passive form of leadership. Deborah's strategic military decisions were crucial to the success of the campaign against Sisera. She didn't merely advise Barak; she actively participated in the planning and execution of the military strategy. Her decision to lead the Israelite army alongside Barak demonstrated exceptional courage and a remarkable willingness to put herself in harm's way to secure the freedom of her people. Her actions contradict the notion that women were inherently incapable of military leadership or participation in warfare. The victory wasn't solely Barak's; it was a collective victory, a triumph of faith and courage led by Deborah's inspired leadership.

The battle itself was a remarkable display of divine intervention. The torrential rains turned the Kishon River into a raging torrent, overwhelming Sisera's army and leading to their utter defeat. This miraculous intervention confirmed Deborah's faith and underscored the power of God's involvement in her leadership. The defeat of Sisera wasn't merely a military victory; it was a spiritual victory, a triumph of faith over fear, of courage over oppression. It was a resounding confirmation that God actively participates in the lives of those who trust Him, empowering them to overcome seemingly insurmountable obstacles.

The song of Deborah, recorded in Judges 5, is a powerful poetic masterpiece that celebrates the victory over Sisera and recounts the events of the war. It's a testament to her faith, her leadership, and the power of God's intervention. The song also highlights the courage and participation of women, both in the battle and in the support of the Israelite army, challenging the patriarchal interpretations that often minimize women's contributions. Her song is not a self-congratulatory anthem but a praise song to God, acknowledging His sovereign hand in the victory and celebrating the collective effort of the Israelite people.

The story of Jael, who courageously killed Sisera, further exemplifies the collaborative spirit of this campaign. Jael's act of courage, though seemingly brutal, was an act of defiance against an oppressive enemy. It highlights the role of women in times of conflict, demonstrating their willingness to confront evil and defend their people. It's a testament to the strength and courage that God imbues in his daughters when they are called to action. The significance of Jael's actions shouldn't be minimized; she was an integral part of the victory, a crucial element in the overthrow of Sisera's tyranny.

Deborah's legacy extends far beyond the battlefield. Her life serves as a timeless example of faith, courage, and leadership for women of all generations. She stands as a powerful symbol of God's willingness to use women in positions of authority and to empower them to challenge oppressive systems. Her story reminds us that faith and courage aren't confined to specific roles or societal expectations; they are gifts available to all who follow God's will. Her example encourages us to embrace our God-given potential and to step forward in faith, even when facing overwhelming challenges. Deborah's story is not merely a historical account; it is a call to action, an inspiration for every woman seeking to live a life of purpose and impact, guided by faith and empowered by God's grace.

The impact of Deborah's leadership wasn't limited to her own generation. Her story continues to inspire women today to overcome societal barriers and embrace their God-given potential. It challenges the notion that women are inherently less capable than men in leadership roles, and it affirms that God uses women powerfully in His kingdom. Her life serves as a model for women in ministry, in business, in politics, and in all areas of life. It's a reminder that women can be strong leaders, effective strategists, and unwavering champions of justice.

Deborah's life stands as a testament to the fact that God doesn't confine His call to any specific gender or societal expectation. He equips and empowers individuals based on their faith, courage, and willingness to serve. Deborah's life is a powerful example of how God chooses, equips, and utilizes women in extraordinary ways, demonstrating that true leadership is not defined by gender but by faithfulness, courage, and a heart devoted to serving God and His people. Her narrative is a challenge to us all to break free from limiting beliefs, to identify our unique gifts, and to step into the purpose God has uniquely designed for us. It is a story of empowerment, courage, and unwavering faith—a story that resonates deeply with women today and inspires them to rise to their full potential in God's kingdom. This resonates not only with the women of Deborah's time but serves as an ongoing encouragement for women of all generations to embrace their strength and faith, to challenge the status quo, and to step into their God-given purpose with unwavering confidence. Deborah's legacy lives on as a powerful reminder of the divine potential within each of us.

## Breaking Limits

Deborah's story is not simply a historical account; it's a powerful rebuttal to the limited roles society often assigns women. Ancient Israelite society, much like many societies throughout history, was deeply patriarchal. Women held limited power, their roles largely confined to the domestic sphere. Their voices were often silenced, their contributions minimized, and their potential largely untapped. This societal structure, rooted in cultural norms and religious interpretations, created significant obstacles for women seeking to exert leadership or influence. Yet, Deborah, a woman of profound faith and unwavering courage, shattered these barriers, demonstrating that God's call transcends cultural norms and societal expectations.

The very fact that Deborah served as a judge in Israel was a radical act of defiance. The role of judge, demanding wisdom, authority, and decisive action, was traditionally occupied by men. That Deborah, a woman, held this position speaks volumes about her exceptional character and the divine appointment she received. Her authority wasn't merely tolerated; it was acknowledged and respected, indicating a level of acceptance and influence that significantly transcended the limitations imposed by societal norms. The people sought her counsel, recognizing her wisdom and trusting her judgment, illustrating a remarkable departure from the prevalent patriarchal expectations. Her leadership wasn't a fleeting anomaly; it was a sustained period of influence, suggesting a gradual shift in societal understanding or at least an acceptance of God's divine choice.

Navigating a patriarchal society required exceptional courage and strategic finesse. Deborah wasn't naive to the potential backlash or resistance she might encounter. Her actions weren't impulsive but rather deliberate and well-considered. She didn't aggressively challenge the existing power structures head-on, but instead utilized her influence to guide and empower others within the existing framework. By dispensing justice fairly and providing spiritual guidance, she gradually shifted the cultural landscape, subtly challenging the ingrained biases against female leadership. Her actions, rather than words, became her most potent form of resistance and advocacy. She demonstrated the competence of women as leaders through practical example, dismantling the biases with effectiveness rather than direct confrontation.

The interaction with Barak highlights another crucial aspect of Deborah's approach. Barak, though a courageous military leader, hesitated, displaying a lack of confidence and possibly reflecting the societal conditioning of his time. Deborah didn't dismiss or belittle his hesitation but rather guided and encouraged him, strengthening his faith and bolstering his resolve. Her leadership style was not autocratic but empowering. She didn't dictate but inspired, demonstrating the importance of collaboration and mentorship. This approach, focused on building up others, speaks to her understanding of true leadership – not about wielding power but about fostering growth and enabling others to reach their potential. It was a significant strategic move: by successfully leading through Barak, she simultaneously achieved victory and demonstrated the capability of women to effectively lead men.

The battle itself, though miraculous in its divine intervention, further challenged prevailing societal norms. Deborah's participation in the military campaign alongside Barak is exceptionally noteworthy. Warfare was largely a masculine domain, and a woman's involvement in such a capacity was unheard of or at least highly unconventional. Her presence on the battlefield was not just symbolic; she played an active role in the planning and execution of the military strategy, demonstrating exceptional strategic acumen and courage. Her actions directly countered the limited roles assigned to women in society and provided a powerful example of female competence in a field traditionally dominated by men. The victory, achieved through a combination of faith, strategy, and divine intervention, served as a potent testament to her leadership and the capabilities of women.

The song of Deborah, often overlooked in the broader narrative, offers further insight into the societal context. It's more than a celebration of victory; it's a social commentary. The song itself highlights the participation of women in the war effort, naming and praising their contributions. It implicitly acknowledges their crucial role in the victory, which directly contradicts the patriarchal narrative that often relegated women to supporting roles. The song acts as a counter-narrative, highlighting the significant contributions and leadership of women—actively challenging the prevalent societal limitations. It's a powerful reclamation of women's agency, celebrating their courage, resilience, and active participation in the liberation of their people. It's a testament to Deborah's commitment to visibility and social change, ensuring the narrative included the silenced voices of her sisters in faith.

While secondary to Deborah's narrative, the story of Jael further underscores the challenge to societal expectations. Jael's actions, though unconventional and arguably violent, were an act of defiance, a stark challenge to the established power structures. Her involvement highlights the willingness of women to take radical action to protect their people, thereby challenging the portrayal of women as passive victims. Jael's role served not just as an instrumental component in the victory but as an emblem of female empowerment and resilience, illustrating that women were not passive observers but active participants in shaping their destiny. Her actions served as a powerful illustration that women were not limited by societal restrictions.

Deborah's legacy extends far beyond her lifetime. Her story serves as a powerful example for women facing similar challenges today. The obstacles to leadership and influence faced by women often still exist, albeit in different forms. Gender bias remains prevalent in many sectors, with women facing subtle and overt discrimination. Deborah's life demonstrates that it is possible to overcome these challenges through faith, courage, and a steadfast commitment to God's calling. Her story inspires women to challenge limitations, embrace their unique strengths, and step into their God-given purpose with unwavering faith, confidence, and determination.

The lessons from Deborah's life are timeless and transcend cultural boundaries. Her leadership was marked by wisdom, courage, and a profound trust in God's guidance. Her legacy continues to inspire women to break free from societal expectations, challenge limiting beliefs, and embrace their full potential. She serves as a reminder that God calls women to leadership roles, empowering them to effect positive change in the world. Deborah's journey is not just a story of the past; it's a roadmap for the present and the future, a testament to the enduring power of faith, courage, and unwavering determination in the face of adversity. It's a call to every woman to rise and embrace their divine purpose, recognizing the inherent strength and leadership potential within them. The challenges may be different, but the spirit of Deborah's courage and faith remains an eternal beacon of hope and inspiration. Her story continues to resonate, empowering women to challenge societal norms, step into their calling, and make their mark on the world. She reminds us that true leadership transcends gender, reflecting instead a dedication to faith, courage, and service to God and His people.

Deborah's life, though lived centuries ago, resonates powerfully with the experiences and challenges faced by women in leadership today. Her story is not merely a historical account; it's a timeless blueprint for navigating the complexities of authority, influence, and spiritual discernment in a world that often undervalues or undermines the contributions of women. The challenges Deborah faced – societal expectations, political maneuvering, and the daunting task of leading an army – find parallels in the contemporary struggles faced by women striving for leadership positions in various spheres of life, whether in business, ministry, community organizations, or even within their own families.

One of the most significant parallels lies in the subtle and overt resistance women often encounter when stepping into positions of authority. Deborah's leadership was not readily accepted; she faced skepticism and opposition from both men and, potentially, women who held to traditional societal roles. Similarly, today, women frequently encounter resistance, often masked as constructive criticism or veiled in professional etiquette. This resistance can manifest in various forms: microaggressions that dismiss their ideas, the subtle undermining of their contributions in meetings, the overlooking of their expertise in favor of male colleagues, or even overt challenges to their authority. Deborah's unwavering resolve in the face of such resistance serves as a powerful reminder that leadership often necessitates enduring such obstacles with grace and unwavering conviction.

The courage Deborah displayed in confronting Sisera and his army reflects the courage necessary for women to navigate the often-hostile environments of leadership. This courage isn't merely about bravery in the face of danger; it's the courage to speak truth to power, to challenge the status quo, to advocate for justice and equality, and to persist despite setbacks and criticism. It takes courage to challenge ingrained biases, to question outdated systems, and to refuse to accept the limitations imposed upon women. In today's world, this courage might be demonstrated by a woman leading a crucial project and overcoming resistance from male colleagues, a female pastor confidently addressing her congregation despite potential backlash, or a woman in a political role fiercely advocating for policies that benefit marginalized communities.

Deborah's leadership wasn't solely about commanding an army; it was about inspiring and empowering others. She didn't operate in isolation; she collaborated with Barak, recognizing his strengths and leveraging his abilities to achieve their shared goal. This collaborative approach is crucial for effective leadership in any context. Women in leadership roles must foster collaboration, build strong teams, and empower others to contribute their unique talents and perspectives. Instead of viewing others as competitors or threats, they must create environments where individuals feel valued, respected, and empowered to share their ideas and contribute their strengths. This involves active listening, providing constructive feedback, and delegating tasks effectively, all of which are crucial for building a strong and successful team.

Furthermore, Deborah's example highlights the importance of strategic planning and decisive action. Her victory wasn't accidental; it was the result of careful planning, shrewd decision-making, and decisive execution. Similarly, successful leadership in today's world requires strategic thinking, the ability to analyze situations effectively, and the capacity to make informed decisions under pressure. This includes the ability to set clear goals, develop effective strategies, allocate resources wisely, and anticipate potential challenges. It requires the discernment to choose the right battles, to prioritize tasks effectively, and to make tough decisions when necessary. It is in this ability to strategically plan and decisively act, mirroring Deborah's actions, that modern female leaders can find their strength.

Deborah's reliance on prayer and spiritual discernment is a crucial aspect of her leadership that remains highly relevant today. Her leadership was not solely based on tactical prowess; it was deeply rooted in her faith and her trust in God's guidance. This spiritual foundation provided her with the resilience, the wisdom, and the courage to lead her people through incredibly challenging circumstances. For modern women in leadership roles, this emphasis on spiritual grounding is equally important. In the face of overwhelming pressures, burnout, and constant demands, a deep spiritual connection provides the strength, perseverance, and resilience necessary to sustain effective leadership over time.

Still Needed Today

In today's fast-paced and demanding world, the spiritual practices that sustained Deborah are even more critical. Regular prayer, Bible study, and meditation provide a source of peace, guidance, and strength amidst the chaos. The practice of seeking wisdom and counsel from trusted mentors and advisors, another key element of Deborah's approach, is also vital for navigating the challenges of leadership. A strong support system can provide encouragement, accountability, and wise counsel, helping women to overcome obstacles and make informed decisions. This mentorship network is not solely for spiritual guidance; it provides a critical sounding board for strategic and professional matters as well.

The modern woman in leadership should emulate Deborah's example by fostering a deep connection to their faith, seeking spiritual guidance, and nurturing strong relationships with mentors and peers. This spiritual foundation is not just a personal pursuit; it informs and strengthens their leadership. This spiritual grounding equips them to lead with integrity, compassion, and wisdom, overcoming challenges with grace and determination.

Deborah's leadership, however, was not without its complexities. While the Bible celebrates her achievements, it also acknowledges the challenges she faced and the complexities of her decisions. This honesty is important for contemporary women. Leadership is not without its difficulties; it demands sacrifice, perseverance, and the capacity to handle criticism and opposition. Understanding that challenges and difficulties are inherent parts of leadership allows women to approach these challenges with resilience and determination.

Moreover, the legacy of Deborah is not solely about her own achievements; it's about the legacy she left for future generations of women. Her story inspires women to step into positions of leadership, to overcome obstacles, and to make a positive impact on the world. Her life serves as a testament to the power of faith, courage, and collaborative leadership. By embracing the principles embodied in Deborah's life, women today can make significant contributions to their communities and to the world, leaving behind a legacy of strength, wisdom, and grace. Her story is a powerful affirmation of the divine potential within every woman, a call to embrace our God-given gifts and talents, and to use them to serve others and to build a better world.

The application of Deborah's example to today's world extends beyond specific leadership roles. It speaks to the inherent strength and capabilities within every woman. Her story is a powerful rebuke to limiting beliefs and societal norms that seek to confine women to secondary roles. It's a call to every woman to recognize her intrinsic value, her potential for leadership, and her ability to make a significant impact in the world. This impact may not always be on a grand scale; it can be found in the quiet acts of leadership within a family, a community, or a workplace. The spirit of Deborah lives on in every woman who dares to step into her God-given purpose, who embraces challenges with courage, and who leads with wisdom, faith, and grace. Her legacy is a powerful encouragement for women to embrace their strength, to claim their place in leadership, and to use their gifts to build a world where every woman's voice is heard and valued.

Deborah's story isn't just about a military victory; it's a profound lesson in the power of a woman's voice, a voice often silenced or marginalized throughout history and even today. Finding your voice in leadership, as Deborah demonstrated, isn't about shouting down others; it's about speaking truth with grace, clarity, and unwavering conviction. This requires a journey of self-discovery, a process of understanding your unique strengths, and cultivating the assertiveness needed to navigate the complexities of leadership.

The first step in finding your voice is acknowledging its existence. For many women, societal conditioning and ingrained cultural expectations have led to a silencing of their inherent power. We've been taught to be quiet, agreeable, and deferential, traits that can be detrimental to effective leadership. Deborah, however, shattered those expectations. She didn't hesitate to speak directly to Barak, a military leader, challenging his hesitancy and offering strategic guidance. This act of assertive communication, though seemingly simple, was revolutionary for its time.

This necessitates a critical self-reflection. What are your unique strengths and talents? What passions drive you? What injustices ignite your fire? Understanding your core values and beliefs provides the foundation for your voice. It allows you to articulate your vision with conviction and to connect with others on a deeper level. Discovering your voice requires honesty, self-awareness, and a willingness to embrace vulnerability. It means acknowledging your limitations alongside your strengths. It's in the recognition of these facets of self that a truly authentic voice emerges. This honesty, this vulnerability, is often the most powerful tool in your leadership arsenal.

It's vital to differentiate between assertive communication and aggression. While Deborah was assertive, she wasn't aggressive. She didn't resort to personal attacks or belittling others. Instead, she communicated her ideas with clarity and respect, even when faced with opposition. This balance—firmness without hostility—is crucial for effective leadership. It's the ability to speak your truth without silencing or dismissing the voices of others. It requires empathy and understanding. Consider Deborah's relationship with Barak. She didn't command him; she collaborated with him, recognizing his strengths while also assertively guiding the course of action. This demonstrates the power of collaboration and mutual respect.

Developing assertive communication requires practice. It's a skill that is honed over time through consistent effort and self-reflection.

Start small. Practice expressing your opinions in situations where the stakes are relatively low. Gradually, increase the challenges you face, practicing expressing your views in more demanding situations. Seek feedback from trusted friends, mentors, or colleagues. Their insights can be invaluable in helping you refine your communication style and develop greater confidence. This practice isn't solely about verbal communication; it encompasses written communication as well. Consider how you communicate in emails, reports, or presentations. Is your voice clear, concise, and confident? Or is it hesitant and uncertain? Honest self-assessment is crucial.

Assertiveness in leadership extends beyond simply stating your opinions; it involves advocating for yourself and others. Deborah stood up for the Israelites, leading them in battle against a powerful oppressor. This involved not only strategic planning but also the courage to challenge the existing power structures and fight for justice. This advocacy requires emotional intelligence. Understanding the dynamics of your environment is critical. You must be able to read the situation, anticipate potential challenges, and adjust your approach accordingly. Consider what levers you can pull to effect change, and how you can best work within the constraints of the situation.

In today's world, this might involve advocating for equal pay, challenging discrimination, or speaking out against injustices within your workplace or community. It might mean mentoring younger women, guiding them in their leadership journeys and helping them find their own voices. It could also involve standing up for those who cannot speak for themselves. It's about using your voice not just for your benefit but for the benefit of others, much as Deborah used her influence to defend and liberate her people.

The process of finding your voice requires courage. It's challenging to step outside your comfort zone, to challenge the status quo, and to speak up against those who may disagree with you. However, this courage is essential for effective leadership. Deborah's example illustrates that confronting opposition is not only possible but necessary for achieving lasting change. This is where your faith and spiritual grounding are integral. Prayer, meditation, and spiritual disciplines will bolster your courage and allow you to remain grounded in your faith even during intense opposition. Draw strength from your faith to build resilience and persevere through inevitable setbacks.

This courage, however, should not be mistaken for recklessness. Finding your voice isn't about being confrontational or aggressive. It's about speaking your truth with grace and respect, even when it's difficult. It's about balancing assertiveness with empathy, understanding that your voice is powerful but should be used to lift up others, not to tear them down. This is where grace comes into play, tempering the strength of your voice with kindness and understanding.

Deborah's story demonstrates that finding your voice is a lifelong journey. It's a process of continuous growth, learning, and adaptation. It's about refining your communication skills, developing emotional intelligence, and cultivating the courage to speak your truth with conviction and grace. It's a journey of both self-discovery and self-acceptance. It's about embracing the imperfections, the vulnerabilities, and the strengths that make you uniquely you. Embrace the journey, celebrate the victories, and learn from the setbacks. The path to finding your voice, like Deborah's journey to leadership, is often challenging but ultimately rewarding. Your voice matters; use it wisely and well. The world needs to hear it. Your unique perspective, your faith, and your experiences are essential contributions to the world around you. Do not underestimate the impact you can have. Speak your truth, empower others, and let your voice echo with grace, courage, and unwavering faith.

## Discussion Question

1. What does Deborah's story in Judges 4 and 5 reveal about the role of women in leadership according to the biblical narrative?

2. How does Deborah's leadership challenge societal norms and expectations of women's roles during her time?

3. In what ways did Deborah demonstrate her strategic acumen and military leadership during the campaign against Sisera?

4. What significance does Deborah's role as both a prophetess and a judge have in the context of Israel's oppression under Jabin's rule?

5. How does Deborah's interaction with Barak reflect her ability to empower and encourage others, particularly men, in their God-given roles?

6. What does the imagery of Deborah sitting under her palm tree symbolize regarding her leadership and accessibility to the people?

7. How does the miraculous intervention during the battle against Sisera illustrate the relationship between faith and divine guidance in Deborah's leadership?

8. In what ways does Deborah's story serve as a source of inspiration for women today, particularly in contexts where they face oppression or marginalization?

9. What themes are present in the song of Deborah in Judges 5, and how do they highlight the contributions of women during the battle?

10. How can Deborah's actions and leadership challenge contemporary interpretations of women's roles in religious and societal contexts?

# CHAPTER 3

## JAEL: COURAGE IN UNEXPECTED PLACES

Jael's story, unlike Deborah's, unfolds not on the battlefield but within the quiet confines of a tent. It is a story of courage that is both startling and profoundly inspiring, a testament to the unexpected ways God can use even the most unlikely individuals to accomplish His purposes. While Deborah's leadership was overt and commanding, Jael's was clandestine, a shadow in the night that brought about the decisive blow against Sisera and his Canaanite army. Her actions challenge our understanding of courage, demonstrating that bravery doesn't always manifest in grand gestures but can be found in the quiet resolve to confront evil, even when faced with overwhelming odds.

The Book of Judges recounts Jael's encounter with Sisera, the commander of Jabin's army, with stark simplicity. Sisera, fleeing from the disorderly retreat of his forces at the hands of Deborah and Barak, sought refuge in Jael's tent. Exhausted and desperate, he asked for water and shelter, a plea seemingly impossible to refuse based on the cultural norms of hospitality prevalent in that time. Yet, Jael, a woman whose name signifies "ibex" – a creature known for its agility and surefootedness – didn't simply offer sanctuary. She acted with a decisiveness that bordered on audacious. While

Sisera slept, she drove a tent peg through his temple, effectively ending his life and the threat he posed to the Israelites.

This act, seemingly brutal by modern standards, must be understood within its historical context. The Canaanites were not merely enemies; they were ruthless oppressors, worshippers of Baal, and perpetrators of unspeakable cruelty. Years of subjugation had left the Israelites weary and demoralized. Sisera, as their military leader, symbolized this oppressive regime. His death was not simply a personal act of vengeance; it was a symbolic end to the era of Canaanite dominance, a turning point in the Israelites' struggle for liberation.

Jael's action is often met with mixed reactions. Some see her as a heroic liberator, a woman who dared to act decisively where others hesitated. Others view her act as cold-blooded murder, questioning the morality of her actions. The complexities of her situation, the weight of her decision, are often overlooked in these simplistic interpretations. This is where theological reflection becomes essential. God, throughout scripture, often chooses the unexpected, the seemingly insignificant, to accomplish great things. Think of David, the shepherd boy who defeated Goliath, or Moses, the former prince who led his people out of slavery. Jael, in her unexpected act of courage, fits within this divine pattern.

Her courage wasn't born out of bravado or a thirst for blood. It stemmed from a deep-seated faith, a belief in the righteous cause of her people, and a willingness to take a stand against overwhelming odds. She had the opportunity to follow the cultural dictates of hospitality, safeguarding her own life and remaining neutral in the conflict. Yet she chose a different path, a path fraught with danger and potential repercussions. She risked everything – her reputation, her life, her family's safety – to act in obedience to what she perceived as God's will, mirroring other women in scripture who acted decisively for the sake of their people, such as Esther who risked her life to save her people. This decision, born from faith, transcended the ordinary constraints of her time.

The narrative surrounding Jael's act is also a powerful reminder of the often-overlooked role of women in biblical history. Women are frequently portrayed in supportive roles: wives, mothers, and sisters. However, Jael's story shatters this stereotype. She is not a passive observer; she is an active participant, a key player in the liberation of her people. She displays an agency and power that challenges the patriarchal structures of her time and ours. Her actions serve as a powerful counterpoint to the pervasive narrative that relegates women to positions of subservience.

Furthermore, Jael's story underscores the importance of recognizing courage in unexpected places and forms. Courage is not always about facing down an enemy on a battlefield. It can be found in the quiet acts of defiance, in the seemingly insignificant choices that have profound consequences. Jael's courage lay in her willingness to challenge the established norms of her society, to act against the dictates of safety and self-preservation, to place her faith in God's plan even when the consequences were uncertain. This is a powerful lesson for women today who are often faced with similar choices: to remain silent or to speak out, to conform or to resist, to prioritize safety, or to embrace risk.

This quiet courage requires a deep understanding of one's convictions and a willingness to embrace the uncertainty that comes with acting on those convictions. Jael didn't have the luxury of a battle plan or the support of an army. She had only her faith, her quick wit, and her determination. Her story inspires us to consider the times when we have been presented with choices that required courage, but perhaps we chose the easier path, the safer option. Her narrative challenges us to explore our willingness to embrace action in the face of fear. What are the seemingly small acts of defiance that could have a profound impact on our lives and the lives of those around us?

The implications of Jael's actions continue to resonate through centuries. Her story serves as a testament to the power of faith, the strength of women, and the unexpected ways God can use individuals to accomplish His will. Her narrative challenges us to re-evaluate our understanding of courage, prompting us to look beyond the grand gestures of heroism and to consider the quieter, more subtle acts of defiance that can shape the course of history. It is a reminder that God's calling can be found in the most unexpected places, in the most unlikely individuals, and that even seemingly small acts of faith can have an immeasurable impact. Jael's legacy is not only one of military victory, but of a quiet strength that continues to inspire women to embrace their potential for courageous action. It is a strength born of faith and tempered by a profound understanding of the cost of freedom. Her story, therefore, should not be judged solely on the act itself, but rather on the context, the faith, and the profound consequence of her decision. It is a story that calls us to consider the courage we might find within ourselves, waiting to be unleashed for God's glory.

The story of Jael, a seemingly insignificant woman from the fringes of Israelite society, serves as a potent illustration of God's propensity to utilize the unexpected to achieve His purposes. Her narrative transcends the simple recounting of a military victory; it becomes a profound theological reflection on divine intervention and the power of faith in the face of overwhelming odds. The seemingly brutal act of killing Sisera, the Canaanite commander, was not merely an isolated event but a pivotal moment in the liberation of Israel, a turning point orchestrated by a God who chooses the unexpected and often the seemingly unlikely, to bring about His will.

Consider the biblical account itself. Deborah, the prophetess and judge, led the Israelite army to victory against Sisera's forces. Yet, it was Jael, a woman not mentioned in military strategies or known for any significant political power, who delivered the final, decisive blow. This seemingly insignificant act became a monumental turning point in the conflict, effectively ending Sisera's reign of terror and breaking the Canaanite stranglehold on the Israelites. God did not use the mighty armies or powerful leaders to accomplish the final victory. Instead, He used a woman in a tent, wielding a tent peg. This stark contrast highlights God's unpredictable methods and His ability to work through the most unassuming of agents.

This concept resonates deeply with the Christian faith. Throughout scripture, we see a repeated pattern of God selecting individuals who appear wholly unprepared for the tasks He sets before them. Moses, a stammering shepherd, was chosen to lead the Israelites out of slavery. David, a humble shepherd boy, defeats the giant Goliath, proving that God's power transcends human limitations. These stories, alongside Jael's, demonstrate that God doesn't choose based on human merit or capabilities, but according to His own sovereign will. He often chooses those who are overlooked, underestimated, and seemingly unqualified, to showcase His power and demonstrate that His strength is perfected in weakness (2 Corinthians 12:9).

This theological principle extends far beyond the ancient world. Contemporary examples abound, highlighting God's ongoing practice of using ordinary people to achieve extraordinary things. Consider the quiet acts of faith that transformed movements: The early Christians, persecuted and marginalized, spread the gospel across the Roman Empire, demonstrating the power of faith-driven action in the face of overwhelming opposition. The Civil Rights Movement saw countless individuals, from ordinary citizens to religious leaders, risk their lives and livelihoods to fight for justice and equality, demonstrating that faith in the face of injustice can ignite significant social change.

Similarly, countless individuals today, seemingly ordinary in their daily lives, are conduits of God's grace and transformative power. A single act of kindness, a word of encouragement, a prayer offered in desperation—these seemingly small acts, inspired by faith, ripple outward, touching lives and producing results far beyond what any individual could accomplish alone. A teacher who patiently mentors a struggling student, a volunteer who dedicates their time to serving the needy, a parent who persistently prays for their child's salvation—these actions, born from faith and driven by God's love, echo Jael's quiet yet powerful act of faith.

The narrative of Jael also compels us to consider the nature of courage itself. It's not always the loud, boisterous act of defiance that defines true bravery. Jael's courage was quiet, subtle, a decisive action taken in the stillness of the night. Her act required immense faith and courage. She had to overcome the cultural norms of hospitality and risked the safety of her own family to take a definitive stand. Her courage lay in her willingness to act, to choose faith over safety, obedience to God over self-preservation. This type of courage resonates profoundly with many women today who often face similar internal battles, wrestling with the tension between conformity and defiance, between safety and the call to faith-driven action.

Jael's story forces a re-evaluation of traditional notions of heroism. Often, heroic actions are portrayed as grandiose displays of power, physical strength, or military prowess. Jael's act, however, was a quiet, strategic maneuver, a calculated risk taken in the shadows. This unconventional heroism highlights the fact that God works in mysterious ways and often chooses the seemingly weakest instruments to accomplish the greatest feats. It is a powerful message for women, often relegated to supporting roles in many narratives, that their contribution, though it may appear quiet or understated, can be profoundly significant.

The seemingly contradictory aspects of Jael's actions—the hospitality offered initially followed by the decisive, violent act—invite deep reflection. Her initial offering of water and shelter aligns with the ancient customs of hospitality, yet her subsequent act is seen by many as a brutal and unforgivable act. This duality underscores the complexity of the situation and the challenging moral dilemmas that believers frequently encounter. It challenges us to consider the complexities of faith-based action within specific cultural and historical contexts. While judging actions solely on 21st-century ethical frameworks may seem tempting, we must remember to approach biblical narratives with sensitivity to their historical background.

Jael's story isn't simply about a military victory or a heroic act. It is a deeply theological story, pointing to the unpredictable nature of God's working, the importance of faith-driven action, and the potential for God to use seemingly insignificant individuals to bring about His divine plan. It is a story that challenges us to re-evaluate our understanding of heroism, courage, and faith. It invites us to see God's work at play even in the most unexpected places and through the most unlikely heroes. It is a reminder that even in the stillness of the night, even within the quiet confines of a tent, God's power can be unleashed, transforming history and forever altering the course of a nation.

### Unpredictable God

The significance of Jael's story extends beyond its historical context. It serves as a constant reminder of the unpredictable nature of God's work, His ability to use the ordinary to achieve the extraordinary, and the call to courageous faith in the face of adversity. It challenges us to examine our own lives and to consider how we might be used by God to accomplish His purposes, even in unexpected ways. Are we willing to step out of our comfort zones and embrace the risks involved in living a life of faith? Are we prepared to be used by God, even if it means facing criticism, misunderstandings, or the potential for failure?

Jael's unwavering faith, her quiet courage, and her decisive action all serve as powerful examples for believers today. Her story is a powerful testimony to the unpredictable, yet unwavering, hand of God and His ability to use the seemingly insignificant to accomplish His divine will. It's a compelling narrative that calls us to reflect on the nature of courage, the power of faith, and our own potential to be unlikely heroes in God's grand story. The legacy of Jael is not merely a historical account but a living testament to the transformative power of faith, the unexpected ways in which God works, and the lasting impact of even the seemingly smallest acts of courageous obedience. It challenges us to listen carefully for God's call and to be willing to step into our God-given purpose, even when the path is unclear and the outcome uncertain. For in the most unexpected places, in the hearts of the seemingly insignificant, resides the very power of God Himself.

Jael's story, however, extends beyond a mere recounting of a courageous act; it delves into the profound depths of obedience. Her obedience wasn't a passive acceptance of orders but a conscious, deliberate choice—a decision born from faith and fueled by a deep understanding of God's will, even if that will lead her down a path shrouded in uncertainty and potential danger. This active, faith-filled obedience is a cornerstone of spiritual strength, a principle echoed throughout scripture and profoundly relevant to the lives of women today.

The strength found in obedience isn't about blind adherence to rules or a rigid adherence to tradition. It's about aligning one's will with God's will, understanding that His plan, though often mysterious and unpredictable, ultimately leads to a greater good. Jael didn't understand the full scope of God's plan, but she trusted the divine impulse that led her to act. She didn't question Deborah's instructions; she simply obeyed. This unquestioning obedience, rooted in faith, became the wellspring of her strength, enabling her to overcome fear, overcome cultural norms, and ultimately achieve what seemed impossible.

This type of obedience necessitates a deep relationship with God, a consistent practice of prayer and seeking His guidance. It requires a willingness to listen to the still, small voice, even when that voice contradicts societal expectations or personal comfort. Jael's obedience wasn't born from blind faith but from a connection to God that allowed her to discern His will amidst the chaos of war. Her decision to shelter Sisera, initially an act of hospitality dictated by cultural norms, was subsequently redirected by a higher power, demonstrating the evolving nature of obedience and its capacity to adapt to unforeseen circumstances.

Consider the numerous examples in scripture of individuals whose obedience, however difficult or seemingly illogical, led to remarkable outcomes. Abraham's obedience to God's command to sacrifice his son Isaac, a testament to unwavering faith, highlights the depth of devotion demanded by true obedience. Though ultimately spared, Isaac's near sacrifice underscores the profound trust required when aligning one's will with God's. The profound impact of Abraham's obedience resonates throughout generations, reminding us that genuine obedience stems from a faith that transcends human understanding. Similarly, Joseph's unwavering obedience to God's plan amidst years of unjust imprisonment paved the way for his eventual elevation to a position of immense power and influence in Egypt. His story is a powerful illustration of how obedience, even in the midst of suffering, can lead to unexpected blessings.

The obedience required by God isn't always easy; in fact, it often requires us to step outside our comfort zones and embrace the unknown. It necessitates confronting our fears, challenging our preconceived notions, and resisting the urge to cling to the familiar. Jael's actions showcase this profound truth. Her decision to kill Sisera, an act of violence, was undoubtedly outside her comfort zone, challenging the cultural norms of hospitality and respect for guests. However, it was through this act of courageous obedience that she ultimately played a decisive role in securing the victory for Israel. Her decision highlights the fact that God sometimes calls us to make difficult choices, requiring a level of obedience that demands sacrifice and courage.

This concept of obedience extends beyond the grand narratives of scripture. It touches the daily lives of countless women today, often in subtle, unassuming ways. It's the single mother who chooses to persevere despite overwhelming odds, driven by a faith that assures her of God's provision and guidance. It's the teacher who tirelessly invests in the lives of her students, fueled by a sense of calling and obedience to a higher purpose. It's the woman who chooses forgiveness over resentment, surrendering her hurt and anger to God's grace and finding strength in obedience to His command to love her enemies. These women, though often unrecognized, are living testaments to the power of obedience—a power that transcends the historical context of Jael's story and resonates profoundly in the lives of women facing modern-day challenges.

Obedience, however, isn't a passive act; it's an active participation in God's work. It requires discernment, wisdom, and a willingness to discern God's voice amidst the noise of the world. It's not simply about following orders but about actively seeking God's guidance, prayerfully considering the implications of our actions, and trusting His plan even when the path is unclear. Jael's initial act of hospitality could be seen as an act of obedience to cultural norms;

her subsequent act was a redirection of her obedience, demonstrating an active, prayerful response to God's guidance. This nuanced approach to obedience allows for flexibility and adaptation while remaining grounded in unwavering faith.

Furthermore, the obedience that leads to spiritual strength isn't rooted in fear but in love. It's about surrendering our will to God out of a deep love for Him, recognizing His sovereignty, and trusting His ultimate goodness. Jael's obedience wasn't borne from a place of fear but from a deep faith in God and His promise of victory. She understood that her actions, though seemingly small in the grand scheme of things, could profoundly impact the course of history. This understanding, fueled by her love for God and her commitment to His will, gave her the strength to overcome her fear and act decisively.

The narrative of Jael offers a powerful model for women today, challenging them to embrace the strength that comes from obedience. It encourages us to listen for God's voice, to discern His will, and to respond with courage and conviction, even when the path ahead is uncertain and challenging. It reminds us that true strength isn't found in self-reliance but in surrendering to God's plan, trusting in His guidance, and living a life of unwavering obedience. Her story is a beacon of hope, encouraging women to step into their God-given purpose, knowing that a power that transcends human limitations lies in obedience.

Therefore, the strength found in obedience is not merely a passive acceptance but an active engagement with God's plan. It's a courageous step forward, a decision to align one's will with God's, even when it requires sacrifice, courage, and a willingness to step outside the boundaries of comfort. It's a testament to faith, fueled by love and devotion, allowing women to tap into a reservoir of strength beyond their own capabilities. Jael's legacy stands as a powerful reminder of this truth, a beacon of inspiration encouraging women to find their strength in obedience, to embrace God's plan with unwavering faith, and to discover the extraordinary potential within themselves.

In conclusion, Jael's story offers a potent message for contemporary women: obedience, far from being a sign of weakness, is a wellspring of spiritual strength and empowerment. It's not about blind submission but about discerning God's will, actively engaging in His plan, and trusting Him even when the path is difficult. By embracing this principle, women can unlock their full potential, overcome limitations, and step into the remarkable destiny God has designed for them. Jael's unwavering obedience, manifested in her courageous actions, serves as a timeless example of the strength that emerges when faith, obedience, and courage converge. Her story inspires us to actively seek God's will, to listen for His voice, and to bravely obey, knowing that in obedience lies a power that transcends human limitations, empowering us to become agents of God's transformative work in the world. It is a powerful call to action, urging us to embrace the strength found in obedience and to live lives characterized by faith, courage, and unwavering devotion to God's plan. It's a reminder that even in the most unexpected of circumstances, the quiet strength of obedience can lead to extraordinary outcomes, shaping not only individual destinies but also the course of history itself. Jael's legacy, therefore, lives on, not just as a historical account but as a powerful testament to the life-altering potential of unwavering obedience to God's divine will.

## Fear and Faith Battle

Jael's story, however, is not simply a tale of courageous action; it's a profound exploration of the internal battle between fear and faith, doubt and divine conviction. Her willingness to act, despite the inherent risks and the potential for devastating consequences, reveals a deep-seated trust in God's plan—a trust that transcended cultural norms, personal safety, and even the very real threat of death. This unwavering faith forms the bedrock of her courage, a courage that resonates powerfully with women today who grapple with similar internal struggles.

Many women find themselves paralyzed by fear, their dreams and aspirations stifled by a sense of inadequacy or a debilitating lack of self-belief. The fear of failure, the fear of judgment, and the fear of the unknown are powerful forces that can hold us captive, preventing us from stepping into our God-given purpose. But Jael's story offers a potent antidote to these paralyzing fears, revealing how faith can become the catalyst for courage, enabling us to transcend our limitations and embrace the extraordinary potential that resides within each of us.

Jael's initial act of offering hospitality to Sisera, a seemingly innocuous act dictated by societal norms, subtly reveals the presence of fear and doubt. She was, after all, sheltering an enemy, a man responsible for the immense suffering inflicted upon her people. This seemingly contradictory action, however, wasn't a manifestation of weakness but a demonstration of her human capacity for empathy, a capacity often intertwined with apprehension. Her hospitality could have stemmed from a fear of retribution or a deep-seated reluctance to confront the enemy directly. This initial hesitation, however, didn't define her. It was the subsequent shift in her actions, the divine intervention that led her to overcome her apprehension, that truly illustrates the power of faith in conquering fear.

The transition from hospitality to decisive action wasn't abrupt; it was a gradual process marked by prayerful reflection, a time spent seeking divine guidance amidst the complexities of her situation. We can imagine her wrestling with her conscience, the weight of her decision pressing heavily upon her. She had the opportunity to retreat, to allow her initial fear and doubt to dictate her response.

Instead, she chose to seek God's will, allowing His light to penetrate the darkness of her apprehension, guiding her towards a path that demanded both courage and sacrifice.

The process of overcoming fear and doubt is rarely instantaneous; it often involves a series of internal struggles and a gradual building of faith that empowers us to act despite our apprehension. This process requires intentional engagement with God's word, consistent prayer, and a willingness to surrender our anxieties to Him. Jael's story reminds us that seeking God's guidance is not a passive act; it requires active listening, discerning His voice amidst the noise of the world, and trusting His plan, even when it's shrouded in uncertainty.

The transformative power of prayer cannot be overstated. It's in the quiet moments of communion with God that we find the strength to confront our fears and doubts. Through prayer, we surrender our anxieties to a power greater than ourselves, allowing God to fill us with His peace and courage. Jael's silence during her act of hospitality, a silence that could easily have been interpreted as compliance with Sisera, was, in fact, a profound moment of silent prayer, a time spent seeking God's will and receiving the strength to act decisively.

This transition from passive compliance to courageous action underscores the importance of actively listening to God's voice. This isn't merely about hearing words; it's about discerning His guidance, recognizing His leading, and responding obediently. For Jael, it meant listening beyond the immediate circumstances, perceiving the broader implications of her actions, and understanding her role in fulfilling God's plan for the deliverance of His people. This active listening, cultivated through prayer and a consistent relationship with God, is essential for overcoming fear and doubt.

Beyond prayer and active listening, the act of trusting in God's plan is paramount. This is not blind faith but a conviction born from a deep understanding of God's character, His unwavering love, and His promises. Jael's trust was not a naive acceptance of everything; it was a courageous decision to place her life, her reputation, and her future in God's hands, acknowledging His sovereignty and accepting the potential consequences of her obedience. This profound trust, firmly rooted in faith, empowered her to act decisively.

Trusting in God's plan often requires us to step outside our comfort zones, to embrace the unknown and to relinquish control. Jael's act was undoubtedly outside her comfort zone; it involved violence, a transgression against the cultural norms of hospitality, and a profound risk to her own life. Yet, it was through this step of faith, this willingness to embrace the unknown, that she was able to achieve the extraordinary.

Furthermore, Jael's courage wasn't solely a product of individual strength. It was inextricably linked to her connection with Deborah, a powerful female leader who provided guidance and support. Deborah's encouragement, her affirmation of Jael's potential, and her unwavering faith served as a powerful catalyst for Jael's actions. This highlights the importance of community and support in confronting fear and doubt. Surrounding ourselves with people who believe in us, lift us up in prayer, and encourage us to trust in God's plan is essential for overcoming our anxieties.

The support of a faith community, a network of women who understand and share our struggles, offers invaluable encouragement and guidance. Sharing experiences, mutual support, and collective prayer provide a source of strength that enables us to confront our fears with courage and confidence. Jael's story highlights the empowering nature of sisterhood within the faith, demonstrating the profound impact that community can have on our spiritual journey.

Finally, Jael's story underscores the importance of recognizing and celebrating the courageous actions of women throughout history and in our own lives. Her act of courage, often overlooked in the grand sweep of biblical narratives, serves as a powerful reminder of the significant contributions that women have made to God's kingdom. This recognition empowers us to embrace our own potential, to step into our God-given roles with confidence, and know that our actions, however small they may seem, can have a profound impact on the world around us.

In conclusion, Jael's victory over fear and doubt wasn't a result of inherent bravery but a conscious decision to trust in God's plan, seek His guidance, and act with unwavering faith. Her story serves as a beacon of hope for women today, reminding us that the strength to overcome our fears and doubts resides not in ourselves but in God's unwavering love and His empowering presence. By embracing prayer, cultivating active listening, trusting God's plan, and seeking support from our faith community, we can step into our God-given destinies with courage, confidence, and unwavering faith, emulating Jael's legacy of courageous obedience. Her story is a powerful reminder that even in the most unexpected circumstances, faith can conquer fear, transforming ordinary women into agents of God's transformative power in the world. It's a call to action, urging us to unleash the potential within ourselves, knowing that through faith and courage, we, too, can rise with grace.

## Seizing Opportunities

Jael's story, however, extends beyond the immediate narrative of confronting Sisera. It speaks volumes about seizing unexpected opportunities, those moments when God's hand is clearly evident, even if the path forward isn't immediately clear. Her initial act of hospitality, while seemingly innocuous, paved the way for her courageous act. It was an unexpected opportunity—a chance encounter that transformed into a divine appointment. It challenges us to examine our own lives, to consider the seemingly insignificant moments that might hold the key to unlocking our God-given potential.

How often do we dismiss the everyday occurrences as mundane, failing to recognize the potential for divine intervention? We may overlook the chance meeting, the unexpected phone call, the seemingly insignificant request, all of which might be God's way of leading us toward a significant purpose. Jael didn't actively seek out the opportunity to kill Sisera; the opportunity presented itself within the seemingly ordinary act of hospitality. Her willingness to engage with the unexpected and embrace the uncertainty ultimately allowed her to become an instrument of God's justice.

This willingness to embrace the unexpected is a crucial element of spiritual growth. It requires a conscious decision to step outside our comfort zones, to relinquish control, and to trust in God's guidance, even when the path ahead is unclear. It involves faith, not simply a belief in God's existence, but a trust in His sovereign plan for our lives, a trust that enables us to navigate the uncertainties with confidence. It is a surrender to the divine will, a commitment to following God's leading wherever it may lead.

Consider the numerous times we may have missed opportunities due to our own hesitations or fears. Perhaps we declined a speaking engagement, fearing public speaking. Or maybe we didn't volunteer for a ministry role, clinging to our comfort zone. We might have avoided a difficult conversation, paralyzed by fear of confrontation. These missed chances might have been divinely orchestrated paths toward greater spiritual growth and service. Jael's story serves as a powerful reminder that God often works through unexpected opportunities, often disguised as the seemingly insignificant.

Embracing the unexpected isn't about recklessly charging ahead without discernment. It's about cultivating a posture of receptivity, a willingness to be led by the Spirit. It's about prayerfully discerning God's will, seeking wisdom and guidance through His Word, and listening attentively for His gentle promptings. It's a delicate dance between trusting in God's plan and exercising wise judgment.

Jael's story is a testament to the importance of prayerful discernment. Before she acted, she likely spent time in prayer, seeking God's direction, weighing the potential consequences of her actions. She didn't act impulsively; her decision was a calculated risk born out of faith and a conviction that she was fulfilling God's purpose. The silence she maintained while Sisera slept wasn't an absence of action, but a time of deep spiritual communion, a time of seeking divine affirmation and receiving the strength for the task ahead.

The concept of divine appointments underscores the idea of embracing the unexpected. These are not coincidences; they are moments orchestrated by God, opportunities that arise seemingly out of nowhere, opening doors to incredible possibilities. They challenge us to move beyond our comfort zones, to trust in God's timing, and to respond with obedience, even when we don't fully understand His plan.

How can we cultivate a mindset receptive to these divine appointments? It begins with a posture of humility, a willingness to admit our limitations, and an acknowledgment that God is in control. It requires a deep dependence on God's grace and strength to carry us through the challenges we face. It involves cultivating a spirit of obedience and a willingness to follow God's leading, even when it leads us into unfamiliar territory.

Furthermore, the act of embracing the unexpected often requires a level of vulnerability. We must be willing to expose ourselves to potential risks, to step outside our protective shells and venture into the unknown. Jael's actions were undoubtedly risky; she could have easily been killed by Sisera or punished for her transgression against the norms of hospitality. Yet, her vulnerability became a strength, a testament to her faith and trust in God's protection.

This vulnerability, however, should not be equated with recklessness. It's about being open to God's leading and recognizing that He can work through our perceived weaknesses and vulnerabilities. It's about releasing the need for control and trusting in God's sovereignty, acknowledging that He is ultimately in charge of the outcome. It is a conscious decision to move beyond self-reliance and embrace God's sufficiency.

The unexpected opportunities that God presents are often disguised as challenges, difficulties, or setbacks. Though painful, these experiences can be powerful opportunities for growth, refinement, and deepening faith. Jael's action wasn't easy; it required immense courage and a willingness to risk her life and reputation. Yet, it was through this challenging experience that she demonstrated her unwavering faith and played a pivotal role in God's plan for the deliverance of His people.

We can learn to embrace these unexpected challenges by focusing on God's presence in the midst of adversity. It's in these moments that we experience the transformative power of His grace, His ability to turn our weaknesses into strengths, and our struggles into testimonies. It's an opportunity for growth, strengthening our faith, and deepening our trust in God.

Embracing the unexpected often means stepping outside the parameters of our comfort zones and venturing into uncharted territories. God often leads us beyond our perceived capabilities, expanding our horizons and strengthening our faith muscles. It's a testament to God's transformative power, His ability to take us from ordinary situations to extraordinary outcomes, just as he did with Jael.

Moreover, embracing the unexpected requires cultivating a spirit of gratitude. We must learn to appreciate the small things, the everyday blessings that God showers upon us. Even seemingly insignificant events can hold significant meaning within the context of God's larger plan. It's in recognizing God's hand in the mundane that we begin to see His glory in the extraordinary. Gratitude opens our eyes and hearts to perceive the opportunities God places before us.

Finally, remember that you are not alone in this journey. The support of a strong faith community is essential in embracing the unexpected. Sharing our experiences, praying together, and encouraging one another creates a safe space where we can feel empowered to step outside our comfort zones and trust in God's leading. Jael's success was not solely a product of individual courage but was facilitated by Deborah's guidance and the broader context of the Israelite army.

Jael's story serves as a compelling illustration of how God uses unexpected opportunities to accomplish His purposes. By cultivating a posture of receptivity, prayerful discernment, and trust in God's sovereignty, we can equip ourselves to seize these opportunities, transforming seemingly mundane circumstances into moments of divine intervention, reflecting His glory in the world. It is a call to action, an invitation to step beyond the limits of our perceived capabilities and into the boundless possibilities that God has in store for us. Our willingness to embrace the unexpected will determine the extent to which we participate in God's extraordinary plan for our lives.

## Discussion Questions

1. How do the varying interpretations of Jael's actions reflect the complexities of moral judgment in biblical narratives?

2. In what ways does Jael's story challenge traditional gender roles in the context of her time?

3. What significance does Jael's act of courage hold within the larger narrative of women's roles in scripture?

4. How can Jael's decision to act against cultural norms be viewed as an expression of faith?

5. What parallels can be drawn between Jael's actions and those of other biblical figures, such as Esther or David?

6. How does the portrayal of Jael enhance our understanding of the theme of divine choice in scripture?

7. In what ways might Jael's story inspire contemporary discussions about women's agency and empowerment?

8. How does the theological reflection on Jael's actions impact our understanding of God's use of unexpected individuals in fulfilling His plans?

9. How does Jael's narrative prompt us to reconsider the role of women in biblical history and in modern society?

10. In what ways does Jael exemplify courage and conviction in the face of danger, and how can this be applied to present-day challenges?

# CHAPTER 4

# RUTH: LOYALTY AND FAITHFULNESS

Ruth's story, nestled within the tapestry of the Old Testament, resonates with a profound simplicity and a breathtaking depth of loyalty. It's a narrative that transcends its historical setting, speaking directly to the human heart's capacity for unwavering commitment and selfless devotion. While Jael's story highlighted seizing unexpected opportunities, Ruth's journey underscores the power of unwavering loyalty, a loyalty that stemmed from a deep-seated faith and a profound understanding of what true commitment entails.

The book of Ruth unfolds not on a grand battlefield, but in the intimate context of family and community, a setting that magnifies the impact of Ruth's choices. Her story begins with loss and uncertainty, a backdrop that serves to heighten the significance of her resolute loyalty to Naomi, her mother-in-law. Naomi, having experienced the devastating loss of her husband and both sons, is returning to her homeland, Bethlehem, a place synonymous with sorrow and despair in her heart. Ruth, a Moabite woman, could have easily chosen a different path; she could have returned to her own people, to the familiar comforts of her homeland, leaving Naomi to bear her burden alone. But Ruth's actions defy expectation. She makes a choice—a choice that speaks volumes about her character and her faith.

Her iconic declaration, "Where you go, I will go, and where you stay I will stay. Your people will be my people and your God my God" (Ruth 1:16), is not merely a sentimental expression; it's a solemn oath, a commitment forged in the crucible of loss and uncertainty. It's a testament to a love transcending cultural boundaries and familial ties. Ruth's loyalty isn't a passive acceptance of Naomi's circumstances; it's an active participation in her journey, a shared burden willingly carried. She leaves behind everything she knows—her family, her culture, her gods—to embrace a new life, a life of uncertainty and potential hardship, with a woman who has become her anchor.

The significance of Ruth's decision cannot be overstated. In a society governed by rigid social structures and deeply ingrained cultural norms, her choice was radical and unprecedented. The Moabites were considered outsiders, even enemies, by the Israelites. For a Moabite woman to choose to align herself with a grieving widow, a woman of a rival culture, was an act of extraordinary courage and unwavering devotion. This wasn't merely a matter of politeness or social convention; it was a deliberate rejection of comfort and security in favor of unwavering loyalty and a nascent faith.

Ruth's loyalty wasn't merely an act of kindness; it was a demonstration of faith. Her embrace of Naomi's God—the God of Israel—suggests a growing awareness of a higher power, a power that transcends cultural divisions and offers hope amidst despair. Her act is a poignant portrayal of spiritual transformation, a movement from an unknown deity to the covenant God of Abraham, Isaac, and Jacob. This transition wasn't a superficial conversion; it was a profound internal shift, a testament to the transformative power of faith and the allure of a compassionate and loving God.

The journey to Bethlehem was not easy. It was a journey into the unknown, a path fraught with challenges and uncertainties. Ruth and Naomi faced poverty, hunger, and the social stigma associated with their status as widows. Yet, Ruth persevered, her commitment to Naomi unwavering. She worked tirelessly in the fields, gleaning barley to provide for their sustenance, exhibiting diligence and humility in the face of adversity. Her labor wasn't merely a means to survival but a demonstration of her unwavering dedication to Naomi's well-being.

The narrative of Ruth's gleaning highlights another critical aspect of her loyalty—her diligence and her humility. She didn't demand special treatment or expect preferential consideration. She worked alongside other women, performing the back-breaking work necessary to provide for their survival. This act of humble service underscores the depth of her loyalty; it wasn't conditional on Naomi's reciprocation or on the ease of their circumstances. It was a selfless commitment grounded in love and faithfulness.

Her encounter with Boaz, a wealthy landowner, further illustrates her faith and character. Ruth's respectful and submissive approach to Boaz shows not only her grace and modesty but also her understanding of the cultural norms and her willingness to navigate them with tact and dignity. She doesn't demand assistance; she requests it humbly, exhibiting a profound understanding of societal expectations and a desire to honor them while still securing her livelihood.

Boaz's response, marked by kindness and protection, underscores the divine hand at work in Ruth's life. His actions showcase God's favor upon Ruth and Naomi, a testament to the blessings that often accompany unwavering loyalty and faithfulness. Boaz's recognition of Ruth's character and her devotion to Naomi serves as a powerful affirmation of her righteous actions and unwavering commitment.

Ruth's story isn't just a historical narrative; it's a powerful allegory for the Christian life. Her unwavering loyalty to Naomi mirrors the Christian's unwavering loyalty to Christ. It's a call to commit wholeheartedly to our faith, to stand firm in our beliefs, even when faced with adversity or uncertainty. Just as Ruth left behind everything she knew to follow Naomi, we too are called to leave behind the comforts of the world to follow Christ.

Moreover, Ruth's story emphasizes the importance of selfless service and humble dedication. Her actions remind us that true loyalty isn't about self-preservation or personal gain; it's about putting the needs of others before our own, embracing sacrifice and working tirelessly for the well-being of those we love. Like Ruth, we are called to be servants, to offer our time, our talents, and our resources to those around us, demonstrating our love through acts of kindness and compassion.

Ruth's journey also reminds us of the power of faith in the face of uncertainty. She didn't know what the future held, but she trusted in God's providence and relied on Naomi's guidance. She demonstrated her faith not only through her words but through her actions, through her unwavering commitment and her relentless dedication. Her story serves as an inspiration to us all, demonstrating that faith is not merely a belief system but a way of life, a guiding principle that shapes our decisions and determines our actions.

Finally, Ruth's story highlights the redemptive power of love and loyalty. Her unwavering devotion to Naomi leads to a happy ending, a testament to the blessings that often follow when we commit ourselves to serving others. Through her loyalty, Ruth finds a new family, a new home, and a new beginning. Her story is a powerful reminder that love, loyalty, and faith often intertwine, producing unexpected blessings and leading to a life filled with purpose and meaning. It serves as a model of faithful living that continues to inspire and challenge believers across centuries. Ruth's life exemplifies the transformative power of unwavering loyalty, a powerful testament to the strength of faith, the grace of God, and the enduring beauty of selfless devotion. Her legacy continues to resonate, reminding us of the profound impact of choosing faithfulness even in the face of seemingly insurmountable odds. Her story is an enduring testament to the transformative power of God's love and the enduring legacy of a life lived in unwavering loyalty.

## Community Matters

The enduring power of Ruth's story lies not only in her individual strength and unwavering faith but also in the profound kinship she shared with Naomi. Their relationship serves as a powerful testament to the strength found in meaningful connections, a strength that transcends cultural differences and societal expectations. It highlights the vital role community plays in sustaining us through life's trials and tribulations, offering a lifeline of support and encouragement when we feel most vulnerable. Naomi, burdened by loss and despair, finds solace and companionship in Ruth's unwavering loyalty. Ruth, in turn, discovers a sense of belonging and purpose in her dedication to Naomi. Their bond is a powerful illustration of the transformative power of mutual support and the enduring strength of human connection.

Ruth's decision to follow Naomi wasn't a mere act of obligation; it was a choice born out of genuine love and compassion. It was a recognition of the deep human need for connection and belonging, a need that transcends cultural differences and personal circumstances. In a world often characterized by individualism and self-reliance, Ruth's story reminds us of the importance of valuing relationships and nurturing meaningful connections. It challenges us to consider the depth of our own relationships and to examine how we offer support and receive it in return. Are we actively seeking out meaningful connections, or are we allowing ourselves to become isolated and alone?

The strength Ruth and Naomi found in their kinship wasn't simply emotional; it was practical as well. Their shared struggles, their mutual reliance, and their collaborative efforts to survive hardship fostered a bond of resilience. They faced poverty, hunger, and social ostracism together. They worked together, gleaning in the fields, sharing the meager resources they managed to acquire. This shared experience forged an unbreakable bond, demonstrating the power of collective action and the resilience born from shared adversity. Their story reminds us that we are not meant to navigate life's challenges alone. We are called to support each other, to share our burdens, and to find strength in the unity of our relationships.

Think of the countless women throughout history who have found strength in the kinship of sisterhood. From the women who supported each other during the suffrage movement to the mothers who rallied together to raise their children, the power of collective action and shared experiences has been a constant source of strength. These women instinctively understood the importance of community and the support that comes from sharing our burdens with others. They found solace in their shared struggles and inspiration in each other's resilience. Ruth and Naomi embody this enduring truth, showcasing the resilience born from shared struggles and the enduring strength of human connection.

The importance of kinship extends beyond the immediate family. It encompasses our wider community, our friends, our church family, our colleagues – anyone with whom we share a meaningful connection. These relationships offer us a network of support, a source of encouragement, and a sense of belonging. They provide us with a place to share our joys and sorrows, our hopes and fears, and to receive the empathy and understanding we need to navigate life's challenges. In today's fast-paced, individualistic world, it's easy to become isolated and disconnected. But the example of Ruth and Naomi reminds us of kinship's crucial role in our lives.

The support and strength found within kinship are not merely emotional; they have tangible consequences. Studies have shown that strong social connections are linked to better physical and mental health. People with strong support networks tend to live longer, healthier lives. They are better able to cope with stress, and they are less likely to experience feelings of isolation and loneliness. The practical assistance provided by kinship can also make a significant difference in our lives, particularly during times of hardship or crisis. A helping hand, a listening ear, or a simple act of kindness can be the difference between success and failure, between hope and despair.

The lessons from Ruth's story extend far beyond the historical context of ancient Israel. They resonate with a timeless truth that applies to women across cultures and generations. The enduring power of kinship remains a vital source of strength, providing support, encouragement, and resilience in the face of adversity. In a world that often emphasizes independence and self-reliance, it is crucial to remember the value of community and the strength that comes from meaningful relationships. It is through these connections that we find our truest selves, discover our potential, and learn to navigate life's challenges with grace and resilience.

The book of Ruth is not just a story about loyalty; it's a story about the power of community, the strength found in kinship, and the transformative power of shared experiences. Naomi and Ruth's story reminds us that we are not meant to walk this journey alone.

We are called to connect with others, to nurture meaningful relationships, and to find strength in the bonds that unite us. This interconnectedness, this deep sense of belonging, is essential for our well-being, our spiritual growth, and our ability to thrive in a world that often feels overwhelming and isolating.

Just as Ruth found strength and sustenance in her relationship with Naomi, we too can discover the transformative power of genuine connection. By actively cultivating meaningful relationships, by nurturing our friendships and community ties, and by offering our support to others, we can unlock a wellspring of strength and resilience that will carry us through life's inevitable challenges. The example of Ruth and Naomi reminds us of the profound truth that our deepest strength lies not in our individual abilities, but in the power of our shared humanity and the unwavering bonds of kinship. Let us embrace the lessons of their story and discover the enduring strength that comes from belonging to a loving and supportive community.

We are called, as women of faith, to create and nurture these communities of support. We are called to be Ruths to others, offering our unwavering loyalty and compassion, and to be Naomis, receiving support and sharing our burdens. This requires intentionality. It requires actively seeking out meaningful relationships, nurturing those connections, and being willing to offer support and receive it in return. It means being present for others, listening attentively, and offering a helping hand when it is needed. It's about creating a safe space where women can be vulnerable, can share their struggles without judgment, and can find strength in the collective wisdom and support of their community.

The building of such communities requires effort and dedication. It demands a willingness to step outside of our comfort zones and to invest time and energy in nurturing our relationships. It means showing up, even when it's difficult, being there for others in times of joy and sorrow, and offering unconditional love and support. It necessitates recognizing that we all have something valuable to contribute and that the strength of the community is only as strong as its weakest link. By actively participating in our communities, offering our gifts and talents, and seeking out opportunities for connection, we can create a powerful network of support that will enrich our lives and the lives of others.

Building these communities also requires humility. We must be willing to admit our weaknesses and ask for help when we need it. We must be open to receiving support from others and to acknowledging that we cannot do it all alone. Humility allows us to break down barriers and embrace our shared humanity, recognizing our interdependence and the importance of mutual support. This humility fosters trust and creates a safe space for vulnerability, allowing us to connect with others on a deeper level and experience the transformative power of shared struggles and collective triumphs.

Finally, building supportive communities requires faith. It requires trusting that God is present in our relationships, guiding our interactions, and providing the strength we need to navigate challenges. It requires believing in the power of prayer, the importance of forgiveness, and the transformative potential of grace. By grounding our communities in faith, we create a space where we can experience God's love and support, strengthening our bonds and enriching our lives in countless ways.

**"Loyalty is the cornerstone of any strong relationship."**

Ruth's story is a powerful reminder of the strength we find in kinship, the importance of community, and the transformative power of shared experiences. May we all be inspired by her example, striving to build strong, supportive communities where women can find strength, encouragement, and the unwavering love and support they need to navigate life's journey with grace and resilience. Let us emulate Ruth's loyalty and Naomi's wisdom, fostering genuine connections and building communities that reflect the love and compassion of Christ. May we all experience the abundant blessings that flow from belonging to a loving and supportive community.

Ruth's journey, however, is not solely defined by her loyalty and the strength of her kinship with Naomi. It is equally, if not more so, a testament to her unwavering faith and perseverance in the face of overwhelming adversity. Her story is a profound lesson in trusting God's plan, even when the path ahead seems shrouded in uncertainty and hardship. Leaving behind everything she knew— her home, her family, her familiar culture—to follow Naomi into a foreign land required an extraordinary act of faith. This wasn't a blind leap into the unknown; it was a deliberate choice, rooted in a deep trust in a power greater than herself. It was a recognition that God's hand was guiding her steps, even if she couldn't see the full picture.

This trust wasn't passive; it was active. It wasn't simply believing in God's existence; it was believing in God's provision and guidance. It manifested in her diligent work in the fields, gleaning barley, not simply to survive but also as an act of faith—a trust that God would provide for her needs. Her actions demonstrate a profound understanding of God's character: a God who cares for the vulnerable, who provides for His children, and who works through even the most challenging circumstances. This active faith wasn't devoid of hardship; it embraced it, seeing it as an opportunity for growth, for reliance on God, and for a deepening of her spiritual relationship with Him.

The book of Ruth doesn't shy away from depicting the harsh realities of Ruth's life. Poverty, hunger, and social isolation were her constant companions. She was a foreigner in a land where she didn't speak the language, didn't know the customs, and didn't have a support system beyond Naomi. Yet, amidst these hardships, her faith remained unshaken. Her perseverance wasn't fueled by stubbornness or denial of her circumstances but by an unwavering belief in God's goodness and His ability to work through any challenge. This is a vital lesson for us today. We often face our own trials—financial difficulties, relational struggles, health issues, or feelings of isolation and discouragement. Ruth's story teaches us that we don't have to navigate these challenges alone. We can, and should, lean on our faith, trusting that God will see us through.

Ruth's story is a powerful example of the transformative power of prayer. While the text doesn't explicitly detail her prayers, we can infer that she spent time in communion with God, seeking guidance and strength. Prayer wasn't merely a ritual for her; it was a lifeline, a source of comfort, and a conduit for receiving divine wisdom and support. Her unwavering faith suggests a consistent practice of prayer, a consistent dialogue with her Creator, a consistent seeking of His will and guidance. In our own lives, we can emulate Ruth's example by dedicating time to prayer, seeking God's guidance in our daily decisions, and relying on Him for strength and courage in the face of adversity. Prayer is not a magic wand that instantly removes our difficulties; rather, it is a powerful tool that strengthens our faith, deepens our relationship with God, and equips us to navigate challenges with grace and resilience.

The act of gleaning itself embodies Ruth's perseverance and trust in God's provision. It was hard, backbreaking work, yet she performed it with diligence and unwavering commitment. She didn't complain or become discouraged; she saw it as a means of survival, an opportunity to provide for herself and Naomi. This highlights the importance of active faith—a faith that is not just belief but also action. It is a faith that puts our beliefs into practice, trusting that God will bless our efforts and provide for our needs. This active faith is a powerful antidote to passivity and apathy. It empowers us to take steps, however small, to improve our circumstances and to trust that God will work through our efforts.

Another significant aspect of Ruth's perseverance is her humility. She never demanded anything; she simply worked diligently, accepting whatever came her way. She didn't resent her circumstances; she adapted to them, finding ways to contribute and to make the best of her situation. This humility is essential in cultivating a strong relationship with God. Pride and self-reliance often hinder our ability to receive God's blessings and His guidance. Humility, on the other hand, opens our hearts to receive His grace and His provision. It allows us to acknowledge our limitations and to depend on Him for strength and direction. Ruth's humility serves as a reminder that true strength lies not in self-reliance but in our dependence on God.

Moreover, Ruth's unwavering trust in God is particularly evident in her encounter with Boaz. She showed courage and initiative, approaching him with respect and humility. She didn't expect special treatment; she simply asked for the opportunity to glean in his fields. This demonstrates her faith in God's timing and His ability to provide for her in unexpected ways. Boaz's kindness and generosity are not coincidental; they represent God's provision working through the hearts of others. Her story reminds us that God often works through unexpected people and circumstances to bless His children. It's a lesson in trusting that God's plan will unfold, even if it's not in the way we anticipate.

The culmination of Ruth's journey—her marriage to Boaz and her eventual inclusion in the lineage of King David—is a testament to God's faithfulness and the reward He offers those who persevere in faith. Her story wasn't simply a personal triumph; it was a fulfillment of God's promises, demonstrating the enduring power of His love and His commitment to His people. Her story offers hope and encouragement to us all, assuring us that God sees our efforts, values our faithfulness, and rewards our perseverance. The blessings may not always come in the way we expect, but they will come if we remain faithful, persistent, and trusting in His unwavering love and guidance.

## More than a Story

The lessons from Ruth's life are timeless and profoundly relevant for women today. Her story is not just a historical account; it's a living example of faith, perseverance, and trust in God's plan. In a world that often emphasizes self-reliance and individual achievement, Ruth's story reminds us of the power of dependence on God, the importance of humility, and the transformative effect of unwavering faith. It's a call to action, a challenge to cultivate our own faith, to persevere through difficulties, and to trust in God's unwavering love and support, regardless of the circumstances.

Her story offers practical applications for our own lives. When we face challenges, we can remember Ruth's diligence in the face of hardship, her humility in her interactions with others, and her unwavering faith in God's provision. We can draw strength from her example, reminding ourselves that God is with us, even in the darkest of times. We can emulate her active faith, taking steps to improve our circumstances while trusting in God's guidance and support. We can cultivate humility, acknowledging our dependence on God and being open to receiving His blessings. We can strengthen our own prayer lives, dedicating time to communion with God and seeking His wisdom and direction in all areas of our lives.

Ruth's unwavering faith wasn't a shield against suffering; it was a companion that carried her through it. It wasn't a guarantee of ease, but a source of strength and resilience. Her story encourages us to embrace our struggles, not as defeats, but as opportunities for growth and deepening our relationship with God. It reminds us that faith isn't about avoiding hardship, but about finding strength in God amidst the storm. It's about trusting that even when we cannot see the path ahead, God's hand is guiding us toward His perfect plan. Her story invites us to cultivate that same faith, that same perseverance, and that same unwavering trust in the God who sees us, knows us, and loves us unconditionally. Her life is a living testament to the power of faith, a powerful reminder that even in the most challenging circumstances, God's love and provision endure.

Finally, Ruth's story is an enduring example of the transformative power of grace. God's grace is not earned; it is freely given. It is undeserved, unearned, and unconditional. Through her actions, faith, and humility, Ruth demonstrated receptivity to God's grace, allowing it to transform her life and shape her destiny. This receptivity to grace is key to overcoming adversity and experiencing the fullness of God's blessings. It's a willingness to accept God's love and provision, even when we feel undeserving. It's a willingness to surrender our own plans and trust in God's perfect timing and perfect will. Just as Ruth experienced the outpouring of God's grace, so too can we experience the transforming power of His love when we humble ourselves before Him and open our hearts to receive His grace. Let Ruth's journey inspire us to embrace God's grace, allowing it to mold us, strengthen us, and guide us on our own paths to faith and fulfillment.

## More than Loyalty

Ruth's story isn't merely a narrative of a woman's unwavering loyalty; it's a powerful illustration of the divine principle: God blesses faithfulness. Her journey, marked by profound loss and uncertain beginnings, ultimately blossoms into a testament to God's abundant reward for those who remain steadfast in their commitment to Him and to those He places in their lives. This unwavering devotion, coupled with her tireless work ethic and humble spirit, paved the way for a series of remarkable blessings, each a tangible manifestation of God's favor.

The blessings Ruth received weren't solely material; they were complete, encompassing every facet of her being. Initially, her faithfulness manifested in her decision to leave behind the familiar comforts of Moab and accompany her mother-in-law, Naomi, back to Bethlehem. This act, born from a profound sense of loyalty and love, also demonstrated faith in a God she was coming to know more deeply. It was a leap of faith, a surrender of her own security for the sake of another, a testament to the power of selfless love divinely inspired. This initial act of faith laid the foundation for the subsequent blessings that would flow into her life.

The act of gleaning in the fields of Boaz is another powerful demonstration of Ruth's faithfulness. Gleaning wasn't simply a means of survival; it was an act of perseverance, a refusal to be overcome by adversity. She worked diligently, not complaining or feeling entitled to anything more than what she earned through her own labor. Her hard work and dedication were not unnoticed by God. It was during this time, amidst the physical toil, that she encountered Boaz, a man who demonstrated God's grace and provision in a tangible way. His actions, in protecting her and ensuring her well-being, were a divine blessing, orchestrated by God's unseen hand.

Boaz's kindness wasn't merely an act of charity; it was a direct consequence of Ruth's faithfulness. His protection, his provision of food, and his subsequent proposal of marriage were all parts of a larger divine plan, a reward for her unwavering loyalty and her steadfast trust in God. This wasn't a coincidence; the scripture paints a picture of divine intervention, subtly guiding events to lead Ruth to a life of comfort and security she had never anticipated.

Boaz's actions were not just acts of kindness but channels through which God's blessings flowed.

The marriage to Boaz wasn't merely a union between two individuals; it was a fulfillment of God's promise, a tangible blessing bestowed upon Ruth for her faithfulness. This union brought her stability, security, and a place within the community. It placed her within the lineage of King David, a remarkable elevation in status that solidified her place in the history of Israel. This unexpected elevation wasn't earned through Ruth's own merit, but through her faithfulness to God's unseen hand and plan.

Furthermore, the birth of Obed, her son with Boaz, was a significant blessing, bridging the gap of Naomi's despair and securing the continuation of Naomi's family line. This blessing held a deeper spiritual significance, demonstrating God's faithfulness in restoring and redeeming. The birth of Obed was not just a personal joy for Ruth; it was an answer to unspoken prayers, a fulfillment of a promise, a testament to the power of God's restorative grace. Obed, in turn, became the grandfather of King David, solidifying Ruth's place in the lineage of the Messiah. This lineage, completely unexpected during the hardships of Ruth's early years, underscores God's long-range plan and the blessings bestowed on faithful service.

Ruth's story is filled with instances that highlight God's meticulous attention to detail, His attentiveness to the hearts of those who are faithful. He doesn't overlook the smallest act of devotion, the quiet commitment to loyalty and perseverance. Every instance, from the initial act of leaving Moab to the birth of Obed, showcases God's active involvement in the lives of those who trust Him. This isn't a passive God who simply watches; He is an active participant in our lives, meticulously weaving together events to bring about His perfect plan for His faithful children.

Ruth's blessings weren't limited to material possessions or social standing. They extended to emotional well-being, restoration of hope, and integration into a new community. She found love, family, and a sense of belonging, all elements that were lacking in her earlier life. These blessings speak volumes about the overall nature of God's grace. His blessings don't just address our physical needs; they encompass our emotional, spiritual, and relational well-being. They restore hope and provide a sense of purpose and fulfillment.

The lessons we glean from Ruth's life are timeless and profoundly relevant to women and men today. Her story serves as a powerful reminder that faithfulness, loyalty, and perseverance are virtues that God richly rewards. In a world that often values immediate gratification and superficial achievements, Ruth's story stands as a beacon of hope, illuminating the path towards a life of purpose and fulfillment through unwavering devotion to God and those He places in our lives. It challenges us to re-evaluate our priorities, reminding us that true blessings are not found in material wealth or worldly success, but in unwavering faith, genuine love, and selfless service.

Understanding that God's blessings are not always immediate or easily recognizable is crucial. Ruth's journey was not without hardship; she faced poverty, hunger, and uncertainty. Yet, her unwavering faith and dedication to God, coupled with her loyalty to Naomi, ultimately led to an abundance of blessings. This reminds us that the path to receiving God's blessings often involves perseverance and faith, even amidst challenging circumstances. It's a testament to God's timing and His ability to work through even the most difficult situations to bring about His perfect plan.

Moreover, Ruth's story underscores the importance of active faith. Her faith wasn't passive but expressed through diligent work, selfless service, and unwavering trust in God's provision. This active faith is what sets her apart, enabling her to receive the abundant blessings bestowed upon her. It's a powerful lesson for us today. We are called not just to believe in God, but to actively live out our faith in tangible ways, demonstrating our devotion through our actions and decisions.

In essence, Ruth's narrative is an inspiring tale of transformation, showcasing the powerful influence of God's grace on a life surrendered to His will. Her story speaks to our hearts, prompting reflection on our own level of devotion and commitment, encouraging us to embrace the principles of faithfulness, loyalty, and perseverance, knowing that God, in His infinite wisdom and love, will richly reward our efforts. It's an invitation to examine our lives, to assess the areas where we can strengthen our faith, and to walk confidently into God's plan for our lives, trusting that His blessings, both seen and unseen, will abound for those who remain faithful to Him. Ruth's journey is a living testament to the enduring power of faith, hope, and love, a powerful reminder of God's unwavering commitment to His children.

## Commitment to Loyalty

Ruth's unwavering loyalty extended beyond her relationship with Naomi; it serves as a powerful model for cultivating faithfulness in all our relationships. Her example offers profound lessons for navigating the complexities of love, commitment, and trust in the context of modern life. The principles she embodies – commitment, integrity, selfless service, and unwavering trust – are foundational elements for building strong, healthy, and God-honoring relationships.

One crucial aspect of cultivating faithfulness in our relationships is the conscious commitment to prioritizing our loved ones. Just as Ruth prioritized Naomi's needs above her own, we must actively make a conscious choice to invest time, energy, and emotional resources into nurturing our relationships. This requires intentionality; it's not merely a passive feeling but a deliberate decision to cultivate connection, understanding, and mutual support. This prioritization might involve setting aside specific times for focused interaction, actively listening without judgment, or making sacrifices to meet the needs of our loved ones.

Integrity plays a vital role in fostering faithfulness. Ruth's actions consistently aligned with her words. She demonstrated unwavering honesty and transparency in her dealings with Naomi and Boaz. This integrity built trust, a cornerstone of any strong relationship. In today's world, characterized by a culture of deception and superficiality, cultivating integrity requires a conscious effort to be truthful, transparent, and accountable in our interactions. It means avoiding gossip, being honest even when it's difficult, and striving to maintain consistency between our words and actions.

Selfless service, a hallmark of Ruth's character, is another essential component of faithful relationships. Her tireless work in the fields wasn't driven by self-interest; it was an act of providing for herself and Naomi, demonstrating her unwavering commitment to their well-being. This selfless service reflects a deep love and concern for others, placing their needs before our own. Cultivating this spirit requires a shift in perspective, a willingness to prioritize the needs of our loved ones, even when it means sacrificing personal comfort or convenience. It's about finding joy in serving others, recognizing that genuine love is expressed through acts of service.

Unwavering trust, deeply embedded in Ruth's relationship with Naomi and subsequently with Boaz, is fundamental to cultivating faithfulness. Trust is built through consistent reliability, transparency, and empathy. Ruth's actions consistently demonstrated her trustworthiness, and as a result, she gained the trust and confidence of those around her. In our relationships, nurturing trust requires open communication, vulnerability, and a willingness to forgive. It means being reliable, keeping our promises, and being supportive during times of difficulty. Breaking trust can be devastating; nurturing it requires consistent effort and genuine commitment.

Furthermore, cultivating faithfulness requires forgiveness. Relationships, by their very nature, are imperfect. Disagreements, misunderstandings, and hurts are inevitable. Ruth's story doesn't depict a flawless relationship; it illustrates resilience and forgiveness. Just as Naomi found forgiveness and acceptance within Ruth's unwavering support, we too must learn to forgive our loved ones and ourselves. Forgiveness doesn't mean condoning harmful behavior, but it does mean releasing the bitterness and resentment that can poison a relationship. It requires humility, empathy, and a willingness to extend grace, mirroring the grace God extends to us.

Communication is another vital element in cultivating faithfulness. Open, honest, and empathetic communication forms the foundation of strong, healthy relationships. It requires active listening, the ability to express our needs and feelings without judgment, and the willingness to seek understanding from our loved ones. This involves not only verbal communication but also non-verbal cues, such as body language and tone of voice. Effective communication necessitates creating a safe space where everyone feels heard, understood, and respected. Regular and open communication prevents misunderstandings, promotes intimacy, and fosters a deeper sense of connection.

Furthermore, prioritizing quality time together is critical in nurturing faithfulness. In today's fast-paced world, it's easy to become distracted and allow our relationships to suffer from neglect. Making a conscious effort to spend quality time together, engaging in meaningful conversations and shared activities, strengthens the bonds of love and commitment. This doesn't necessarily require elaborate plans; it can be as simple as sharing a meal together, taking a walk, or engaging in a meaningful conversation. The key is to be present and fully engaged, focusing on connecting with each other rather than being distracted by external factors.

Another crucial aspect of fostering faithfulness is recognizing and addressing conflict constructively. Disagreements are inevitable in any relationship, but the way we handle conflict can either strengthen or weaken the bonds of love and commitment. Cultivating faithfulness involves learning to communicate effectively during disagreements, seeking understanding and compromise, and being willing to forgive. This requires humility, empathy, and a willingness to see the other person's perspective. Conflict resolution should focus on finding solutions that are mutually beneficial, strengthening the relationship rather than tearing it apart. It's about learning to navigate differences with grace and respect.

Beyond the immediate relationship dynamics, cultivating faithfulness involves a commitment to personal growth and spiritual development. Just as Ruth's faith journey underpinned her loyalty and commitment, so too should our own spiritual growth inform our relationships. This involves seeking God's guidance, practicing forgiveness, and striving to live a life that reflects His values of love, compassion, and integrity. Personal growth strengthens our ability to be supportive partners, offering empathy, understanding, and unconditional love. It allows us to address our own shortcomings and to approach relationships with humility and grace.

Finally, the cultivation of faithfulness involves a conscious effort to pray for our relationships. Seeking God's guidance and blessing on our relationships is crucial in fostering loyalty, trust, and understanding. Prayer allows us to align our hearts and minds with

God's will, enabling us to navigate challenges with His wisdom and strength. It's a powerful tool to cultivate humility, empathy and compassion within ourselves, contributing to a deeper level of love and commitment. Prayer also provides a source of comfort and support during times of difficulty, strengthening the relationship through shared faith and reliance on God's guidance.

In conclusion, cultivating faithfulness in our relationships is a continuous journey that requires conscious effort, intentionality, and a commitment to living out the principles of love, integrity, and selfless service. Ruth's example provides a timeless guide for navigating the complexities of love, commitment, and trust, illustrating how unwavering loyalty, born from a deep faith, can lead to abundant blessings. By embracing the principles highlighted in her story, we can build strong, healthy, and God-honoring relationships that reflect the transformative power of grace and the enduring beauty of faithful love. The journey of cultivating faithfulness is a reflection of our journey with God, and as we grow in our relationship with Him, our relationships with others will inevitably flourish.

## Discussion Questions

1. What key themes does Ruth's story illustrate about loyalty and commitment?

2. How does Ruth's decision to accompany Naomi to Bethlehem challenge societal norms of her time?

3. In what ways is Ruth's loyalty portrayed as an active choice rather than a passive response?

4. How does Ruth's declaration of loyalty to Naomi reflect her character and faith?

5. What obstacles did Ruth and Naomi face upon their arrival in Bethlehem, and how did Ruth respond to these challenges?

6. How does the narrative of Ruth's gleaning reflect her diligence and humility?

7. In what ways does Ruth's interaction with Boaz demonstrate her understanding of cultural norms and societal expectations?

8. How is the theme of spiritual transformation represented in Ruth's journey from Moab to Bethlehem?

9. What does Boaz's response to Ruth reveal about his character and the significance of loyalty in the narrative?

10. How does Ruth's story contribute to the larger themes of the Old Testament, particularly regarding faith and devotion?

# CHAPTER 5

# HANNAH: PERSEVERANCE IN PRAYER

Hannah's story, etched within the sacred pages of 1 Samuel, resonates deeply with countless women across generations who have wrestled with the agonizing pain of infertility. Her experience transcends the purely physical; it speaks to the profound spiritual longing for something deeply desired, something seemingly beyond reach. Hannah's persistent prayer wasn't merely a plea for a child; it was a testament to unwavering faith, a demonstration of perseverance in the face of profound disappointment, and a powerful example of how to engage in fervent, heartfelt supplication before God.

Her barrenness, in the cultural context of ancient Israel, was not simply a medical condition; it carried the weight of societal stigma and shame. Childbearing was considered a blessing, a sign of God's favor and a source of familial continuity. To be barren was to be deemed incomplete, lacking in God's blessing, a woman marked by a perceived deficiency. This societal pressure undoubtedly intensified Hannah's emotional burden, adding layers of pain and despair to her already heavy heart. Yet, instead of succumbing to despair, she turned to God in prayer, her heart overflowing with a mixture of sorrow and fervent hope.

The narrative paints a vivid picture of Hannah's emotional turmoil. We see her silently weeping, her heart burdened by her inability to conceive. Her anguish was not a passive resignation but an active, agonizing plea to the Almighty. This internal struggle, this silent cry of the heart, is often overlooked in the recounting of her story. Yet, this very struggle is a powerful illustration of the depth of her faith and the tenacity of her prayer. It reminds us that our struggles, even the ones that feel deeply personal and intensely private, are not unseen by God. He sees the tears that fall unseen and hears the silent prayers uttered in the quiet corners of our hearts.

Hannah's persistent prayer wasn't a fleeting impulse; it was a consistent practice, a deeply ingrained habit woven into the fabric of her daily life. The text doesn't explicitly describe the frequency of her prayers, but the intensity of her plea suggests a continuous communion with God, a persistent seeking of His intervention in her life. This unwavering devotion underscores the power of persistent, consistent prayer – a practice that goes beyond occasional requests and delves into a continuous dialogue with the Divine. It requires discipline, resilience, and unwavering trust in God's timing and His perfect plan. It's a testament to the power of faith that endures beyond the immediacy of answers.

Her prayer at the Tabernacle in Shiloh is especially poignant. Overwhelmed with emotion, she pours out her heart before Eli, the priest. Her words, though few, reveal the intensity of her pain and the desperation of her plea. She doesn't demand; she pleads. She doesn't accuse; she humbly begs for God's mercy. Her silent prayer, initially hidden, transforms into a vocal expression of her deep desire and unwavering faith. This demonstrates a crucial aspect of prayer: sometimes, our prayers are internal, deeply personal cries to God; other times, they require articulation, a vocalization of our needs and desires. Both are acceptable, and both hold power before God.

Initially misinterpreting her fervent prayer as drunken ramblings, Eli speaks to a common misconception about those who pray fervently. Sometimes, our expressions of faith, particularly when laced with intense emotion, can be misunderstood by those who haven't experienced the same depth of longing or desperation. However, Eli's eventual understanding underscores the importance of compassionate listening, even in moments when we might not fully comprehend another's plight. It's a reminder that those who pray intensely, those whose faith is profoundly felt, may often struggle with the outward expression of those feelings. We should approach such expressions with empathy and understanding.

The act of making a vow, promising to dedicate Samuel to God's service if her prayers were answered, speaks volumes about Hannah's faith. It was not a transactional exchange, but rather a heartfelt offering, a gesture of complete surrender to God's will. Her vow demonstrates her unwavering belief in God's power and her willingness to sacrifice for the sake of her desire. This act of devotion illustrates the essence of true faith: a willingness to submit our desires to God's sovereign plan, accepting His will even if it means sacrifice and surrender. This aspect of Hannah's story is crucial for understanding the depth of her faith.

Hannah's perseverance teaches us that unanswered prayers are not necessarily a sign of God's unresponsiveness. Her journey was a prolonged process, filled with waiting, anticipation, and uncertainty. Yet, her faith never wavered. This perseverance in prayer and this steadfast commitment to seeking God's will ultimately led to the fulfillment of her deepest longing. This resonates with countless individuals who grapple with prolonged periods of unanswered prayer. Her story teaches us the importance of enduring faith, of trusting God's timing even when the answer seems delayed or even absent.

The birth of Samuel wasn't merely the culmination of Hannah's persistent prayer; it was the beginning of a new chapter in her life, a chapter marked by faith, gratitude, and a life dedicated to God's service. She fulfills her vow, presenting Samuel to the Lord and devoting him to lifelong service in the Tabernacle. This isn't a story of self-centered gain but of selfless devotion and thanksgiving. It highlights an overlooked key element: the importance of expressing gratitude once prayers are answered. Hannah's dedication of Samuel showcases the heartfelt thankfulness that should accompany answered prayers.

Hannah's story continues to inspire women today because it speaks to the universality of longing, hope, and faith. It speaks to the strength found in perseverance and the power of prayer. Her story isn't simply a historical anecdote; it's a living testament to the transformative power of faith, demonstrating that persistent, heartfelt prayer, coupled with unwavering trust in God, can overcome seemingly insurmountable obstacles. Her experience is a beacon of hope for anyone wrestling with unanswered prayers, reminding us that God hears even the silent cries of the heart, and that perseverance in prayer is a crucial element of our spiritual journey.

Her unwavering faith in the face of adversity, persistent prayer, and ultimate fulfillment of her vow serve as powerful inspiration for women today. She exemplifies the resilience and determination inherent in the feminine spirit, demonstrating that faith, patience, and unwavering dedication to God are potent forces capable of overcoming seemingly insurmountable challenges. Her legacy extends beyond her personal experience, serving as a guidepost for women navigating the complexities of life, faith, and the pursuit of their spiritual destiny.

Further, Hannah's story underscores the importance of community in our spiritual journey. While her struggles were profoundly personal, her eventual triumph was shared with others. The act of bringing Samuel to the Tabernacle, of dedicating him to God's service, was a public expression of faith, an act witnessed by the community. This highlights the crucial role of community support in navigating life's challenges. Our spiritual journeys are often deeply personal, yet the support and encouragement of fellow believers can be instrumental in sustaining our faith and perseverance.

Hannah's story also reveals a crucial truth about God's nature: He sees our hearts, understands our deepest desires and sorrows, and doesn't dismiss our tears or ignore our pleas. Her experience reinforces the truth that God is deeply involved in the details of our lives, even in our pain and suffering. This intimacy with God, this assurance that He is near and intimately aware of our struggles, is a source of immeasurable comfort and hope.

Finally, Hannah's story stands as a powerful example of the transformative power of faith. Her journey from despair and barrenness to joy and fulfillment is a testament to the grace and power of God. Her persistent prayer wasn't simply about receiving a child; it was about encountering God, experiencing His unwavering love and faithfulness, and discovering her purpose in His service. This transformation is a powerful message for all believers: that God's grace can overcome any hardship and that through faith and perseverance, we can find our way to His purpose for our lives. Her legacy is not simply in her son, but in the unwavering faith she demonstrated, a faith that continues to inspire and encourage generations of believers.

**Overcoming the Feelings of Inadequacy**

Hannah's story, while primarily focused on her fervent prayer for a child, offers a profound insight into overcoming feelings of inadequacy that resonate deeply with women today. Her barrenness, a significant societal stigma in ancient Israel, undoubtedly fueled feelings of personal failure and worthlessness. Imagine the weight of societal expectation pressing down on her – the whispers of judgment, the silent condemnation, the feeling of being incomplete, a woman deemed less than because of her inability to bear children. This wasn't simply a medical condition; it was a social and spiritual identity crisis, a deep-seated sense of inadequacy that permeated her being.

This sense of inadequacy wasn't unique to Hannah's time; it's a pervasive experience for women in the twenty-first century. The relentless pressure to achieve the "ideal" – the perfect career, the perfect family, the perfect body – creates a breeding ground for feelings of self-doubt and insufficiency. The curated perfection projected on social media, the constant comparison to others, and the internalized expectations of success often lead to a pervasive sense of falling short, of never quite measuring up. Hannah's struggle, therefore, becomes a powerful mirror reflecting the internal battles many women face today.

Yet, Hannah's response to her feelings of inadequacy is where her story becomes truly transformative. She didn't succumb to despair or self-pity. Instead, she chose a path of faith and persistent prayer. Her prayer wasn't a passive resignation to fate, but an active engagement with God, a courageous confrontation of her deepest fears and insecurities. This highlights a crucial element in overcoming inadequacy: active faith, not passive acceptance. It requires a conscious decision to trust in a power greater than ourselves, a willingness to lay down our burdens and embrace the possibility of grace.

Hannah's prayer wasn't merely a request for a child; it was a cry for validation, for affirmation, for a restoration of her sense of worth. Her silence, her tears, her fervent supplications before God speak to a deeper yearning – a yearning for acceptance, for belonging, for a sense of purpose beyond her perceived shortcomings. In her prayer, she found a space to express her pain, to acknowledge her inadequacy, and to find strength in the face of her struggle. This act of vulnerability, of honest confession before God, is a crucial step in dismantling the walls of inadequacy that confine us.

It's important to note that Hannah's prayer wasn't a one-time event. It was a consistent practice, a daily engagement with God that sustained her through periods of prolonged waiting and uncertainty. This consistency underscores the importance of persistent prayer as a tool for overcoming feelings of inadequacy. It's not enough to pray once and expect immediate results; it's the consistent seeking, the unwavering trust, and the ongoing dialogue with God that cultivates resilience and hope. This lesson applies to all aspects of life: persistent effort, consistent dedication, and unwavering faith are vital for overcoming challenges.

Consider the analogy of a plant struggling to grow in barren soil. A single watering may offer temporary relief, but consistent nurturing, consistent provision of sunlight, and nourishment are what enable it to flourish. Similarly, our spiritual growth and our ability to overcome feelings of inadequacy require consistent engagement with God through prayer, study of scripture, and fellowship with other believers. It's not a sprint; it's a marathon of faith, a persistent striving towards spiritual maturity.

Furthermore, Hannah's experience teaches us the importance of self-compassion in overcoming feelings of inadequacy. She acknowledged her pain, her frustration, and her sense of failure, but she didn't let these feelings define her. She didn't wallow in self-pity; she turned to God, seeking strength and guidance. This self-compassion, this ability to acknowledge our flaws and imperfections without self-condemnation, is essential for healing and growth. We must learn to treat ourselves with the same kindness and understanding we would offer a friend struggling with similar challenges.

Hannah's vow to dedicate Samuel to God's service if her prayer were answered, speaks volumes about her humility and her willingness to surrender her desires to God's will. This act of sacrifice was not a transactional exchange, but a profound expression of faith, a gesture of complete surrender. This willingness to submit to God's plan, even if it involves sacrifice, is essential in overcoming feelings of inadequacy. When we relinquish the need to control every aspect of our lives and trust in God's sovereignty, we find freedom from the self-imposed pressure to be perfect.

The birth of Samuel was not simply the fulfillment of Hannah's prayer; it was a pivotal moment of transformation. It was a tangible manifestation of God's grace, a testament to the power of persistent faith. The act of bringing Samuel to the Tabernacle, of dedicating him to God's service, was an act of public gratitude, a proclamation of God's faithfulness. This public acknowledgment of her dependence on God and his provision serves as a powerful example of how we can overcome the shame and silence often associated with feelings of inadequacy.

Hannah's story, therefore, offers a multi-faceted approach to overcoming feelings of inadequacy. It emphasizes the importance of:

**Persistent prayer:** A consistent, heartfelt communion with God, expressing our struggles, seeking guidance, and trusting in His grace.

**Self-compassion:** Treating ourselves with kindness and acknowledging our imperfections without self-condemnation.

**Surrender to God's will:** Releasing our need for control and trusting in God's sovereign plan, even if it means sacrifice.

**Public gratitude:** Openly acknowledging God's faithfulness and sharing our testimony with others.

These principles, drawn from Hannah's life, are timeless and universally applicable. They offer a pathway to healing and wholeness for women facing feelings of inadequacy, regardless of their specific challenges. Hannah's story becomes a powerful encouragement and a beacon of hope in the ongoing journey towards spiritual maturity and self-acceptance. Her experience is not merely a historical account; it's a living example of God's grace at work, transforming a life marked by perceived inadequacy into one characterized by faith, gratitude, and unwavering devotion.

Her story resonates even more profoundly when we consider the specific cultural and religious context in which she lived. Barrenness was not simply a medical condition; it was a social and religious stigma, carrying the weight of societal judgment and spiritual inadequacy. This adds another layer to Hannah's struggle, highlighting the intersection of personal experience with cultural and religious expectations. It underscores the power of faith to overcome not only personal challenges but also societal and religious pressures that can fuel feelings of inadequacy. Her resilience in the face of such pressures is a powerful testament to the transformative power of faith.

In the modern context, the pressures faced by women often stem from differing sources. The relentless pursuit of perfection, fueled by societal expectations and social media's unrealistic portrayals of success, creates a breeding ground for feelings of inadequacy. The constant comparison with others, the pressure to balance career aspirations with family responsibilities, and the internalized expectations of self-sufficiency can leave many women feeling overwhelmed and insufficient. Hannah's experience offers a vital counter-narrative, demonstrating the power of faith to transcend these external pressures and cultivate an inner sense of worth and purpose.

Her journey from silent weeping to joyful thanksgiving is a powerful symbol of the transformative power of faith. It's a testament to the fact that God sees our deepest struggles, hears our silent cries, and offers grace and healing to those who seek Him. Hannah's story encourages us to embrace our vulnerabilities, to acknowledge our inadequacies, and to trust in God's unwavering love and faithfulness. It's a reminder that societal expectations or our perceived achievements do not determine our worth, but by the inherent dignity and value that God bestows upon each of us. In embracing this truth, we begin to overcome the feelings of inadequacy that can hinder our spiritual growth and fulfillment. Hannah's life becomes a guide, a roadmap for navigating the complexities of faith and finding strength in the face of adversity. It's a powerful reminder that even in our deepest struggles, God's grace is sufficient.

Hannah's unwavering prayer, however, wasn't simply a fervent plea; it was a profound demonstration of humble supplication. This aspect of her prayer, often overlooked amidst the narrative of her barrenness and subsequent miracle, holds a crucial lesson for women today striving to overcome feelings of inadequacy and find solace in God's presence. Humble supplication is more than just asking; it's a posture of the heart, an attitude of dependence that acknowledges our limitations and trusts entirely in God's power and grace.

The Hebrew word often translated as "supplication" carries within it a sense of bowing down, of prostrating oneself before God. It's a posture reflecting a deep awareness of our own insignificance in the face of God's majesty and power. It's a recognition that we are not self-sufficient and that we cannot achieve our desires through our own efforts alone. This acknowledgment of our dependence is the very foundation of humble supplication. Hannah's prayer wasn't a demand or a negotiation; it was a heartfelt cry from a soul desperately seeking God's intervention.

This humility is strikingly contrasted with the prideful spirit that often hinders our prayers. Pride, in its many subtle forms, whispers that we are capable of handling things ourselves and that we don't need God's help. It leads us to rely on our own strength, our own resources, our own clever plans, rather than seeking God's guidance and relying on His power. Pride prevents us from truly opening our hearts to God and from genuinely acknowledging our need for His grace.

**God leads the humble to do what is right and teaches the humble His truths. (Palm 25:9)**

Hannah's experience highlights the detrimental effects of pride in prayer. While the text doesn't explicitly state that she was prideful, her initial silence and inward struggle suggest a sense of self-reliance that initially prevented her from fully embracing God's help. She carried her burden alone for a time, wrestling with her sorrow and despair before finally breaking through into heartfelt supplication. Her journey underlines the crucial shift from self-reliance to God-reliance, a pivotal turning point in her relationship with God. This underscores that genuine supplication emerges from a place of recognizing our limitations, not our capabilities.

Consider the countless times we approach prayer with a sense of self-sufficiency. We meticulously plan our requests, formulating eloquent prayers, outlining our needs with precision and careful articulation. We meticulously strategize the 'right' approach to

God. While such preparation can be beneficial, it can also mask a subtle pride—a belief in our own ability to influence God's will through our meticulously crafted words and actions. This subtle self-reliance can subtly choke the very spirit of humble supplication.)

True humble supplication, as exemplified by Hannah, is characterized by a willingness to lay down our pride and embrace our vulnerability before God. It's about acknowledging our weaknesses and limitations, recognizing that our strength comes not from ourselves, but from God. It is a sincere admission of our dependence upon Him. It's about surrendering our own agenda and aligning our will with His.

This posture of humility isn't about self-deprecation or belittling oneself; rather, it's about recognizing our place within God's grand scheme. It's about acknowledging our limitations while simultaneously embracing the infinite possibilities of God's love and power. It's a posture of complete dependence, of childlike trust, of unwavering faith in a power greater than ourselves.

The power of humble supplication lies in its transformative effect on our hearts and minds. When we approach God humbly, we create space for His grace to flow into our lives. We open ourselves to His guidance and wisdom. We allow Him to work in ways that we could never have imagined. It's in this vulnerability, in this surrender, that we experience the true power of prayer. In this space, God can reveal His boundless love, His unwavering faithfulness, and His extraordinary capacity to heal, restore, and empower.

The transformation in Hannah's life serves as a profound testament to this power. Her initial silent sorrow gave way to a heartfelt cry, a powerful supplication that moved God's heart. Her humility paved the way for God's intervention, resulting in the miraculous birth of Samuel and a profound transformation in her life.

This lesson of humble supplication is particularly relevant to modern womanhood. The pressures of societal expectations, professional ambitions, and personal relationships often lead women to feel overwhelmed and inadequate. We strive for perfection, often forgetting to acknowledge our inherent limitations. This pursuit of self-sufficiency can mask a subtle pride that hinders our prayers and prevents us from experiencing the full power of God's grace.

The constant comparison to others, fueled by social media's curated portrayals of perfection, further exacerbates this sense of inadequacy. We measure our worth against unrealistic standards, overlooking our own unique strengths and contributions. This relentless striving often leaves us feeling depleted, disconnected, and even isolated from God. The antidote to this is humble supplication. It's an invitation to relinquish our relentless pursuit of self-sufficiency and instead, to wholeheartedly embrace our dependence on God's strength and provision.

Humble supplication is not a passive act of resignation; rather, it's an active engagement with God, a courageous embrace of our vulnerability. It requires a conscious decision to relinquish control and trust in a power greater than ourselves. It is a surrender of our self-reliance to divine grace. It invites us to approach God not as a judge or a taskmaster, but as a loving Father who cares deeply for our well-being.

The practice of humble supplication is a lifelong journey, a continuous process of self-examination and surrender. It involves actively seeking God's guidance, humbly acknowledging our mistakes, and persistently seeking His forgiveness. It requires a willingness to be transparent and honest with God, admitting our weaknesses and imperfections. It's a consistent practice that cultivates within us a deeper dependence upon Him.

In addition to prayer itself, the practice of regularly examining our hearts for pride is essential. Pride can be insidious, often masquerading as confidence or ambition. Self-reflection, introspection, and honest self-assessment can help us identify the subtle ways pride manifests itself in our thoughts, words, and actions. Seeking accountability from trusted friends or mentors can also provide valuable insights into blind spots and areas where humility is needed.

The fruit of humble supplication is multifaceted. It brings peace amidst turmoil, strength amidst weakness, and hope amidst despair. It fosters a deeper relationship with God, characterized by trust, intimacy, and unwavering faith. It enables us to experience the transformative power of God's love and grace in a profound and life-altering way.

Hannah's story is a timeless reminder of the power of humble supplication. Her persistent prayer, born out of a humble heart, transformed her life and serves as a beacon of hope for women today. Her journey reminds us that true strength lies not in self-reliance but in our complete dependence on God. In embracing this posture of humble supplication, we, too, can experience the transformative power of God's grace, finding strength and solace in His unwavering love and provision. It is in this surrender, this humility, that we unlock the transformative power of prayer and experience the fullness of God's grace in our lives. And in that, we discover a strength that surpasses all worldly understanding.

## God's Timing

Hannah's story isn't merely about barrenness and the miraculous birth of Samuel; it's a profound narrative about faith, perseverance, and the often mysterious timing of God. While her persistent prayer ultimately resulted in the answer she so desperately sought, the journey itself reveals a crucial truth: God's timing, though sometimes perplexing, is always perfect. The years of waiting, the silent tears, the fervent pleas—all were part of God's intricate plan, a plan that ultimately brought about far more than just a child. It brought about a profound spiritual transformation in Hannah herself and a legacy that echoes through the ages.

Understanding God's timing requires a shift in perspective. It requires us to move beyond our human desire for immediate gratification and embrace a posture of trust in God's sovereignty. We live in a culture obsessed with instant results, where immediate gratification is often prioritized over long-term growth and spiritual maturity. We expect answers to our prayers immediately, often feeling discouraged or even questioning God's faithfulness when our desires aren't fulfilled on our timetable. Hannah's experience challenges this impatient approach. Her years of waiting weren't a sign of God's indifference, but rather an integral part of His process.

Consider the spiritual growth Hannah likely experienced during her years of barrenness. Her pain and longing likely deepened her faith and refined her character. The constant wrestling with her sorrow and longing propelled her to a profound intimacy with God, a closeness that would have been impossible had her prayer been answered immediately. This waiting period, however challenging, was a crucible in which her spirit was refined, her faith tested and strengthened, and her heart prepared for the immense blessing to come.

The delay wasn't a punishment or a denial, but a divinely orchestrated season of preparation. God wasn't ignoring her; He was meticulously preparing her, molding her heart and spirit to receive the gift He had planned for her. This waiting period, this time of testing and refining, shaped her into a woman of incredible faith and resilience, uniquely equipped to raise a son who would become a pivotal figure in Israel's history.

The concept of "Kairos" in Greek illuminates this truth further. Kairos refers to a divinely appointed time, a moment of perfect timing ordained by God. It differs from "Chronos," which denotes chronological time. God works within the framework of Chronos, but He operates according to the principle of Kairos. His actions are not limited by our human understanding of time; He works within His own perfect timing, a timing that often transcends our own limited comprehension.

This is not to say that we should passively wait for God to act, neglecting our own responsibilities and efforts. Hannah's persistent prayer demonstrates that active faith involves consistent seeking, persistent supplication, and unwavering trust in God's plan, even when the answer isn't immediately apparent. Her actions demonstrated faith not simply in *if* God would answer, but *when* and *how* He would answer. Her perseverance in prayer reflects this active faith in the face of uncertainty.

The fulfillment of Hannah's prayer – the birth of Samuel – wasn't merely a happy ending; it was a culmination of a process, a testament to God's faithfulness and His perfect timing. The miracle wasn't just the birth itself, but the transformation of Hannah's life, the spiritual growth she experienced during the waiting period, and the immense impact Samuel would have on the nation of Israel. God's timing ensured that both Hannah and Samuel were fully prepared for the roles they would play in God's grand narrative.

This truth extends beyond Hannah's personal story. Consider the countless women throughout history who have faced prolonged waiting periods, longing for answers to their prayers, grappling with unanswered questions, and enduring periods of uncertainty. Their journeys, often marked by hardship and pain, mirror Hannah's experience. Yet, in the midst of their waiting, God was at work, shaping their character, refining their faith, and preparing them for the blessings He had in store. Their stories are a testament to the power of perseverance, the importance of trust, and the ultimate perfection of God's timing.

Reflect on your own life. Are you currently facing a period of waiting? Are you longing for an answer to a prayer, grappling with an unresolved issue, or enduring a season of uncertainty? Hannah's story offers a powerful message of hope and encouragement. It reminds us that God's timing is not our timing; His ways are higher than our ways, and His thoughts than our thoughts. (Isaiah 55:9)

Though often challenging, the waiting period can be a time of profound spiritual growth. It's a time to deepen our relationship with God, cultivate patience and perseverance, and develop a stronger trust in His sovereignty. During these seasons, we are invited to engage in reflective prayer, actively seek His guidance, and surrender our anxieties to His loving care. It is in this surrender, this unwavering trust that we discover the transformative power of God's timing.

We must actively cultivate patience. Patience is not passive resignation but an active choice to trust God's plan, even when it doesn't align with our expectations. It requires faith, perseverance, and a willingness to wait upon the Lord. This waiting, however, should never be passive. Instead, it should be a time of active engagement with God, of seeking His guidance, and of remaining steadfast in prayer.

The lesson from Hannah is not to passively wait but to actively trust. This means consistently seeking God in prayer, remaining faithful to His word, and actively living out His commands. It's a proactive, not reactive, faith that demonstrates trust, not demanding answers but surrendering to His perfect timing.

Remember, God's timing is not arbitrary; it is purposeful. He works with precision and intention, orchestrating events to fulfill His perfect will in our lives. While we may not always understand His methods or His timetable, we can trust in His unwavering love and His ultimate goodness. Our role is to remain faithful, to persevere in prayer, and to trust in His perfect timing, knowing that His plan is far greater than anything we can imagine. As challenging as it might be, the journey is as much a part of God's plan as the destination. And in the end, the fulfillment of His promises will far surpass our expectations. In embracing this perspective, we find not only peace in the waiting but also a deeper understanding of God's grace and a transformed heart prepared for His perfect timing.

## Steadfast Faith

Hannah's journey, as we've explored, wasn't merely a tale of infertility culminating in a miraculous birth. It's a powerful illustration of unwavering faith in the face of prolonged adversity, a testament to the transformative power of persistent prayer, and a profound revelation of God's perfect, albeit sometimes mysterious, timing. Her story resonates deeply because it mirrors the struggles many women face – the aching longing for something deeply desired, the frustration of unanswered prayers, and the persistent question of "why?" But within her story lies a powerful message of hope and resilience, a message that speaks directly to the heart of every woman navigating difficult seasons.

The essence of trusting God in difficult times isn't about the absence of pain, doubt, or frustration. It's about maintaining a steadfast faith even when our circumstances seem to contradict our hopes and prayers. It's about clinging to the promise of God's love and faithfulness, even when the path ahead seems shrouded in uncertainty. Hannah's persistent prayer wasn't a denial of her pain; instead, it was a declaration of her faith—a testament to her belief that God was bigger than her suffering, that His plan held a purpose beyond her immediate comprehension.

One key aspect of Hannah's faith that stands out is her persistence. She didn't pray once and then give up. Scripture portrays her as pouring out her heart to God repeatedly, year after year. This unwavering persistence speaks volumes about the depth of her faith and her unwavering trust in God's ultimate goodness. She didn't demand answers; she didn't threaten God or question His love. Instead, she persisted in prayer, seeking His presence and strength through the turmoil. This persistent prayer wasn't just a vocalization of her needs; it was an act of worship, an affirmation of her dependence on God, and a continuous seeking of His grace.

This kind of persistence in prayer requires a deep-seated understanding of God's character. Hannah's faith was rooted in the knowledge of a loving, compassionate God, and ultimately in control. She understood that His ways are higher than our ways, His thoughts far beyond our thoughts (Isaiah 55:9). This understanding allowed her to persevere, even when the answers she longed for remained elusive. Despite the years of silence, she held onto this knowledge, reminding us that true faith is not the absence of doubt but perseverance in the face of uncertainty.

Consider the internal battle Hannah must have faced. She lived in a society where barrenness was often equated with a lack of favor from God. The societal pressure, the whispers of judgment, and the silent pain of longing could have easily crushed her spirit. Yet, instead of succumbing to despair, she found solace in prayer and refuge in God's presence. This refuge wasn't passive; it was an active choice—a conscious decision to trust in God's love and plan, regardless of her circumstances.

The process of trusting God during challenging times isn't about magically erasing the difficulties. It's about navigating those difficulties with a profound sense of God's presence and guidance. It's about finding strength not in our own abilities but in the power of God's grace working through our lives. For Hannah, the process was not without its emotional toll, yet she remained steadfast in her faith, revealing the transformative power of persistent prayer.

How do we cultivate this kind of trust and perseverance in our own lives? Firstly, we must cultivate a deeper understanding of God's character. The more we study His Word, the more intimately we know His nature, and the stronger our faith will become. This knowledge, this close relationship with God, is the foundation upon which unwavering trust is built. Through prayer, Bible study, and fellowship with other believers, we come to know God's steadfast love and faithfulness, which anchors our souls during times of storm.

Secondly, we must learn to embrace the process. Difficult seasons are rarely quick fixes. They often require patience, endurance, and a willingness to walk through the valley with God. The waiting period, the unanswered questions, the prolonged struggles—these are not necessarily indications of God's absence but are often integral parts of the refining process. Just as the goldsmith refines gold in the fire, so God refines our hearts through trials, shaping and strengthening our faith.

Thirdly, we must maintain a posture of active faith. This means actively seeking God's guidance, persistently praying, and faithfully living out His commands, even when we don't see immediate results. Hannah's story reminds us that active faith is not passive resignation. It is an unwavering commitment to trust in God's plan, regardless of the length or difficulty of the journey. This active faith is crucial. It is not merely hoping for a positive outcome but a resolute trust in God's presence and purpose amidst the struggle.

Finally, we must remember that God's timing is always perfect. While we may crave immediate answers, God's plan unfolds according to His divine timetable, which often transcends our human understanding. The delay is not necessarily a denial; it can be a crucial part of God's refining process. Hannah's story reminds us that God's timetable often allows for deeper spiritual growth and a more profound transformation than we could achieve in shorter timeframes.

In conclusion, Hannah's story provides a powerful template for navigating difficult seasons. It's a testament to the transformative power of persistent prayer, a demonstration of unwavering faith in the face of adversity, and a profound revelation of God's perfect timing. Her journey reminds us that trusting God in difficult times isn't about the absence of challenges but about facing those challenges with a heart rooted in faith, hope, and an unwavering trust in God's sovereignty. Her persistence serves as a powerful example of unwavering faith and is a beacon of hope for all women facing challenging periods in their lives. By embracing her example, we can learn to navigate our own trials with greater faith, hope, and a renewed perspective on God's perfect timing, knowing that His love and faithfulness endure, even in the deepest valleys.

The story of Hannah resonates across centuries, offering a timeless message of hope and encouragement to every woman who has ever felt the weight of unanswered prayers or the sting of unfulfilled desires. It is a reminder that even in the darkest of nights, the light of God's grace shines through, guiding us on a journey of faith that culminates in a victory far greater than we could ever imagine. The process of trusting God isn't a passive act; it's a constant, active engagement with His plan, a decision to surrender to His will even when it is unclear. This active trust allows us to experience not only the eventual blessing but also the profound spiritual growth and refinement that occurs during the waiting period itself. This is the true heart of trusting God in the midst of difficulties. It is not just about the final outcome but the transformation of the heart that occurs along the way.

## Discussion Questions

1. What societal pressures did Hannah face due to her infertility in ancient Israel, and how did these pressures impact her emotional state?

2. In what ways does Hannah's story illustrate the spiritual longing experienced by many who struggle with infertility?

3. How does Hannah's approach to prayer reflect her deep faith and perseverance in the face of disappointment?

4. What does Hannah's silent weeping reveal about her internal struggle, and how does it relate to the concept of faith?

5. How does the text illustrate the importance of consistent and persistent prayer in Hannah's life?

6. What role does the act of vocalizing prayer, as seen in Hannah's interaction with Eli, play in the process of seeking God's intervention?

7. How does Eli's initial misunderstanding of Hannah's fervent prayer highlight the need for compassion and empathetic listening?

8. In what ways does Hannah's vow to dedicate Samuel to God showcase the essence of true faith and surrender?

9. What lessons can we draw from Hannah's perseverance in prayer regarding the nature of unanswered prayers?

10. How does Hannah's story encourage individuals who are currently experiencing struggles with unanswered prayers or deep longings?

# CHAPTER 6

# ESTER: COURAGE AND STRATEGIC ACTION

Esther's story, unlike Hannah's intimate and personal struggle, unfolds on a grand, almost theatrical stage. While Hannah's battle was waged in the quiet solitude of her heart and home, Esther's courage played out amidst the opulence and intrigue of the Persian court, a world rife with danger and political maneuvering. Yet, both women share a common thread: unwavering faith, expressed in dramatically different ways. Hannah's faith was persistent prayer; Esther's was a calculated, strategic risk taken in obedience to God's unseen hand.

The book of Esther is unique among the biblical narratives. It doesn't explicitly mention God's name, yet His providential hand is evident throughout the story. Esther's obedience is not a vocalized prayer but a calculated action, a silent offering of her life for her people. This makes her story all the more compelling, challenging our assumptions about how faith manifests and how God works in our lives. It showcases a faith that is not passive or resigned but active, strategic, and profoundly courageous.

Consider Esther's position. A Jewish orphan adopted by her cousin Mordecai, she finds herself unexpectedly thrust into the heart of the Persian empire, selected as queen by King Ahasuerus. This elevation, though seemingly fortuitous, places her in a precarious position. She is a Jew in a Gentile court, surrounded by potential enemies and powerful forces beyond her control. The very act of concealing her Jewish identity is an act of obedience, a strategic move that initially preserves her safety but also carries the inherent risk of future exposure. This initial act of calculated obedience sets the stage for her later, even greater act of courageous faith.

The looming threat of Haman's wicked plot to annihilate the Jews adds a layer of urgency to Esther's situation. Mordecai, witnessing the impending genocide, pleads with Esther to intervene. He implores her to approach the king, to use her position of influence to save her people. But this request isn't a simple plea; it's a call to potentially fatal action. To approach the king uninvited was punishable by death. Esther's response is pivotal, not a rash impulsive decision, but a carefully considered and faith-filled choice.

Esther's initial hesitation is not a lack of faith but a realistic assessment of the enormous risk involved. She understood the precariousness of her position and the potentially devastating consequences of failure. She requests time for prayer and fasting, not as a delay tactic but as a crucial period of seeking divine guidance and strength. This highlights the crucial role of spiritual preparation in facing daunting challenges. It shows that courage isn't the absence of fear but the ability to act despite fear, fueled by a deep-seated faith and trust in a higher power.

The act of fasting itself is significant. It is not merely a physical discipline but a spiritual act demonstrating humility and dependence on God. Through fasting, Esther humbles herself before God, acknowledging her limitations and seeking His wisdom and strength. It represents a period of intense spiritual communion, a silent dialogue with God amidst the turmoil and uncertainty. She uses this time not for panicked self-preservation but for focused prayer and seeking direction.

Upon returning to the King, Esther's actions are meticulously planned. Her approach isn't impetuous; it's calculated. She doesn't blurt out her plea immediately; she uses her influence and charm to gain the King's attention and favor, slowly revealing her request. Her strategic approach showcases not only her courage but also her intelligence, her understanding of the political landscape, and her ability to navigate the complexities of the Persian court. Her approach isn't brute force but carefully crafted, utilizing every resource at her disposal, demonstrating that faith can work effectively in even the most challenging environments.

The invitation to the banquet is not merely a social event but a carefully calculated step toward her ultimate goal. This calculated approach showcases a faith that is not passive but actively engaged with the circumstances, using wisdom and strategy to further God's purposes. It reveals a faith deeply interwoven with practical action, a faith that is both powerful and strategic.

Esther's actions in inviting Haman to the subsequent banquet are equally strategic. She uses the opportunity to expose Haman's true character and intentions to the king. This calculated move further highlights the strategic brilliance underpinning her courageous act of obedience. It illustrates that even acts of faith often require skillful planning and calculated execution, demonstrating a faith that is both bold and discerning. She didn't simply pray; she acted, guided by faith and wisdom.

The pivotal moment, when Esther reveals her identity as a Jew and exposes Haman's wicked plot, is a testament to her extraordinary courage. Risking her own life for the sake of her people demands a profound level of faith and a willingness to sacrifice everything for a higher purpose. This moment is not just a demonstration of courage but also of obedience to God's calling.

Her actions highlight a crucial aspect of faith—the willingness to step outside our comfort zones and take risks for what we believe in. Esther's obedience wasn't passive acceptance; it was active engagement, requiring her to confront the dangerous reality of her situation. It was not just a matter of prayer but a calculated, strategic action, using wisdom, strategy, and deep faith to overcome seemingly insurmountable obstacles.

Esther's story doesn't end with a miraculous intervention. It's a narrative of strategic risk-taking, faith-filled courage, and ultimate triumph through calculated action. It shows us that God often works through unlikely people, using their skills and wisdom to achieve His purposes. Esther's faith is not a passive reliance on divine intervention but an active participation in God's plan, a courageous and calculated response to a dire situation.

Furthermore, Esther's story serves as a potent reminder that our faith shouldn't be confined to private devotion. Our faith should lead us to action, to courageously confront injustice and advocate for those who are vulnerable. Her example reminds us that faith without action is sterile, that true faith is expressed through bold, courageous obedience.

The implications of Esther's risky obedience extend far beyond her historical context. Her story challenges us to examine our own willingness to step outside our comfort zones, take risks for the sake of others, and use our gifts and talents to further God's kingdom. It serves as a powerful example of faith in action, reminding us that even seemingly insurmountable obstacles can be overcome with courage, strategic planning, and a deep trust in God's providence.

In conclusion, while Hannah's persistent prayer demonstrates a powerful form of faith, Esther's risky obedience presents a different, equally powerful, model of faith in action. Both women demonstrate unwavering faith in God's plan, even when the path is shrouded in uncertainty. Hannah persevered in silent prayer while Esther strategically navigated a dangerous political landscape. Both illustrate the diverse ways God calls us to express our faith – sometimes in quiet devotion, sometimes in courageous action.

Their stories, though vastly different in setting and circumstance, ultimately offer a unified message of hope, courage, and the unwavering power of faith. They remind us that God's plan is often revealed not in dramatic pronouncements but in the quiet courage of obedience and the strategic application of His gifts, a testament to the multifaceted nature of faith and its ability to empower women to become mighty warriors for His kingdom. The quiet strength of Hannah and the calculated courage of Esther complement each other, offering a powerful tapestry of faith for women navigating life's complexities in the modern world. These are not isolated examples; they are echoes resonating through history, calling us to embrace our own faith, discover our unique strengths, and answer God's call however it may manifest in our lives. Let us learn from these extraordinary women, embracing our own unique journeys of faith and allowing God to empower us to become the mighty warriors He intends us to be.

**Wisdom and Unwavering Faith**

Esther's story, while devoid of explicit divine pronouncements, is a masterclass in navigating treacherous circumstances with wisdom and unwavering faith. Her journey wasn't a passive waiting for God's intervention; it was an active engagement with her reality, a calculated dance through a minefield of political intrigue and mortal danger. Her success wasn't a matter of luck or divine intervention alone but a product of careful planning, shrewd observation, and a courageous willingness to risk everything for her people.

With its opulent façade and simmering undercurrents of power struggles, the Persian court was far removed from the quiet sanctuary of Hannah's prayer. Esther, a Jewish woman in a Gentile kingdom, constantly walked a tightrope, balancing her faith with the demands of her royal position. This delicate balancing act required not only courage but also a keen understanding of human nature and political dynamics. She wasn't merely surviving; she was strategically maneuvering, using her intelligence and position to create opportunities where none seemingly existed.

Consider her initial decision to conceal her Jewish heritage. This wasn't cowardice; it was a strategic maneuver, a necessary precaution to safeguard her position and, ultimately, to allow her to serve as a protector of her people. It was a calculated risk, a silent prayer wrapped in strategic action. It demonstrated a deep understanding of her environment and a willingness to delay gratification for a greater, long-term purpose. This initial act of calculated obedience paved the way for her future acts of bold defiance.

The revelation of Haman's genocidal plot presented Esther with an almost impossible choice. Mordecai's impassioned plea was not just a request; it was a life-or-death ultimatum. Approaching the king uninvited meant certain death. Yet, Esther didn't cower. Her hesitation wasn't a lack of faith but a profound understanding of the stakes involved. She recognized that impulsive action could be disastrous and that a measured, calculated approach was essential.

Her response wasn't immediate action but a period of prayer and fasting. This wasn't a passive retreat; it was an active seeking of divine guidance. In this context, fasting wasn't mere self-denial; it was a spiritual discipline, a humbling before God, a plea for wisdom and strength. It was a time of intense spiritual communion, a silent conversation with the divine, seeking clarity and direction in the face of overwhelming odds. This preparation was crucial, highlighting the importance of spiritual grounding before undertaking significant actions, especially in high-pressure situations.

Esther's subsequent actions were marked by a calculated precision. She didn't storm into the king's presence with accusations; she strategically used her position and influence to gain his favor. The invitation to the banquet wasn't a social formality; it was a carefully orchestrated step towards her ultimate goal, a subtle way to gain the king's attention and plant seeds of doubt about Haman's intentions. This demonstrates that faith isn't always about grand gestures but often about quiet, strategic maneuvering and discerning the right time and way to act.

Her second banquet was even more strategic. By inviting Haman, she created a scenario that exposed his true character and his wicked plot to the king. This was not just courage; it was brilliance, an ability to see beyond immediate danger and employ her intellect and position to expose evil and secure the safety of her people. She utilized her knowledge of the king's personality and the court's dynamics to her advantage, demonstrating a sophisticated understanding of power dynamics and human behavior.

The moment of revelation, when Esther revealed her Jewish identity and exposed Haman's plan, was an act of profound courage. It was a complete surrender to God's will, a willingness to sacrifice her life for the sake of her people. This wasn't a reckless act of defiance but a carefully orchestrated culmination of strategic planning and unwavering faith. It showed that true courage is not the absence of fear but acting despite it, driven by a higher purpose and an unwavering trust in God.

Esther's story isn't just a historical account; it's a timeless parable about the power of faith in action. It demonstrates that faith isn't passive; it's active and strategic and requires wisdom, discernment, and planning. It's about knowing when and how to act, utilizing all available resources, and having the courage to face overwhelming odds.

Moreover, Esther's narrative offers a powerful example of women's leadership in a patriarchal society. Her ability to navigate the complexities of the Persian court and influence the king's decision demonstrates the potential for women to wield power and influence for good, even within challenging societal structures. Her story inspires us to recognize and embrace our own potential for leadership, reminding us that God empowers women to rise and make a difference in the world.

Esther's journey also underscores the importance of using our gifts and talents for God's glory. Her intelligence, her charm, and her strategic thinking were all instrumental in saving her people. Her story encourages us to identify and develop our unique skills and abilities and use them to serve God and others.

Furthermore, Esther's example challenges us to confront injustice and advocate for the vulnerable. Her willingness to risk her life for her people serves as a powerful call to action, urging us to step outside our comfort zones and use our voices to speak out against oppression and inequality. Her bravery reminds us that silence in the face of injustice is complicity.

Finally, Esther's story reminds us that God works in mysterious ways, often through unexpected individuals and circumstances. Her elevation to queen, her ability to influence the king, and her ultimate success were all part of God's providential plan, demonstrating that even seemingly random events can be part of a larger divine purpose.

## Faith in Action

In the final analysis, Esther's story isn't simply a tale of courage; it's a testament to the power of faith in action, a powerful illustration of navigating difficult situations with wisdom, discernment, and unwavering trust in God's plan. Her calculated risks, her strategic actions, and her unwavering faith offer a powerful model for women navigating the challenges of modern life, empowering us to become the mighty warriors God intends us to be, actively engaging in the world around us, and using our God-given gifts to make a real difference. Her story serves as a constant reminder that faith, when coupled with wisdom and courage, can move mountains and overcome seemingly insurmountable obstacles. It's a story that resonates through time, urging us to embrace our own faith, to discover our unique strengths, and to answer God's call with both courage and wisdom.

Esther's life, as recounted in the Book of Esther, wasn't a series of haphazard events; it was a carefully orchestrated symphony of preparation and opportune moments. Her remarkable success in saving her people wasn't merely a stroke of luck or a last-minute divine intervention. Instead, it was the culmination of years of unspoken preparation, coupled with a remarkable ability to discern and seize the opportunities God placed before her. Understanding this dynamic is crucial for understanding not only Esther's story but also our own potential for impacting the world around us.

The initial preparation wasn't flashy or dramatic; it was the quiet, unassuming groundwork that laid the foundation for her future acts of courage. Her upbringing, her faith, and her inherent wisdom were all essential components of this foundational preparation. Growing up within a devout Jewish family undoubtedly instilled in her a deep understanding of her heritage and her unwavering commitment to her people. This instilled loyalty and faith became her bedrock, a source of strength in the face of unimaginable pressure.

It is important to note that Esther's faith wasn't a passive acceptance of fate; it was a living, active relationship with God, nurtured through prayer, adherence to Jewish traditions, and an abiding trust in God's plan, even when that plan was shrouded in mystery. Her commitment to her faith served as the foundation upon which she built her resilience and courage.

Furthermore, her life in Susa, amidst the grandeur and intrigue of the Persian court, was a unique form of preparation. While seemingly a world removed from the simplicity of her Jewish upbringing, this environment provided her with invaluable lessons in political maneuvering, observation, and diplomacy. She learned the nuances of court life, developing a keen understanding of the king's personality, the motivations of those around him, and the subtle power dynamics at play. This keen observation, honed by her immersion in the royal court, became her most potent weapon in the ensuing battle for the survival of her people.

Consider the significance of her becoming queen. This wasn't a chance encounter; it was an opportunity strategically placed within the divine orchestration of her life. While seemingly accidental, it positioned her in a place of immense power and influence. Her beauty, her grace, and her wisdom undoubtedly contributed to her selection, but God's hand is undeniable in opening this door. This position, however advantageous, presented both incredible challenges and unique responsibilities.

This unexpected elevation underscores the importance of being ready when the call comes. God often uses ordinary people in extraordinary ways. Esther's story reminds us to be prepared, not for a specific event, but for the unexpected turns that life may bring. In this context, preparation is not about striving for perfection or anticipating every possible scenario. Instead, it is about developing the character, skills, and spiritual foundation to respond effectively when called upon. This includes cultivating a deep relationship with God, nurturing our faith, and diligently developing our talents.

The arrival of Haman's wicked plot brought Esther's preparation to the forefront. The threat of annihilation of her people forced her to act. Her initial hesitation wasn't weakness; it was prudence, born from an acute understanding of the peril involved. Approaching the king uninvited was a death sentence, a reality she weighed carefully. This wasn't an absence of faith; it was the careful consideration that wisdom dictates. Her decision to act stemmed from her understanding that inaction was equally dangerous. She had to proceed carefully and strategically, using all the skills and knowledge that she had acquired to date.

Esther's response wasn't rash or impulsive. The period of prayer and fasting that followed was not a mere ritual; it was a crucial phase of preparation. It was a time of intense spiritual engagement, a seeking of divine wisdom and strength, a moment where she sought guidance and clarity from God, preparing not just her body but her spirit for the formidable task ahead.

Her calculated approach to the king, the carefully planned banquets, and her eventual revelation were all hallmarks of strategic action born out of the preparation she had undergone. Each step was calculated, and each decision was measured, driven by her faith and an unwavering commitment to her people. This demonstrates that faith isn't always a grand, dramatic display but often a series of quiet, measured steps and strategic maneuvers undertaken with both wisdom and trust in God's guidance.

The story of Esther serves as a powerful reminder of the importance of readiness. Life rarely follows a predictable path. Unexpected opportunities, challenges, and calls to action often appear when we least expect them. Esther's experience teaches us that we must continually prepare ourselves – spiritually, intellectually, and emotionally – for the unexpected. This isn't about living in fear of the unknown, but about actively cultivating the qualities that will allow us to respond effectively and faithfully when God calls us to action.

This continuous preparation involves nurturing our spiritual lives through prayer, Bible study, and fellowship with other believers. It involves honing our skills and talents and using them to serve God and others. It also means actively seeking opportunities to develop our leadership abilities, engaging in situations that push us beyond our comfort zones and force us to grow in wisdom and discernment.

Further, seizing the opportunities God presents is as important as the preparation itself. Opportunity often presents itself disguised as a challenge or a seemingly insurmountable obstacle. Recognizing the opportunity within the challenge is a critical skill. This requires sensitivity to the promptings of the Holy Spirit, a willingness to step outside of our comfort zones, and a faith that allows us to trust in God's provision even when the path forward seems unclear.

Esther did not cower in the face of danger; instead, she saw the opportunity within the threat, recognizing that her unique position could be used to safeguard her people. This discerning vision, coupled with her courage and unwavering faith, enabled her to rise to the challenge and make a profound impact. Her story inspires us to cultivate a similar sensitivity to the opportunities hidden within life's trials, encouraging us to approach challenges with faith, hope, and the unwavering belief that God has a plan, even within the midst of adversity.

The interplay between preparation and opportunity is beautifully illustrated in Esther's life. Her quiet preparation, her faith, and her wisdom enabled her to seize the opportune moments, leading to a remarkable outcome. This emphasizes the importance of cultivating a lifestyle of constant readiness, allowing us to respond faithfully and effectively whenever God calls us to serve. The lessons learned from Esther's narrative are not confined to the historical context of ancient Persia; they resonate deeply with our own lives and experiences, reminding us that God often works through ordinary individuals, using unexpected circumstances to achieve extraordinary purposes.

Therefore, let us embrace the lessons from Esther's life: cultivate a deep and abiding faith, nurture our spiritual and personal growth, seek opportunities to develop our skills and talents, and never underestimate the power of prayer and fasting as avenues of divine guidance. By doing so, we can prepare ourselves to recognize and seize the opportunities that God places before us, becoming agents of His grace and significantly impacting the world. The story of Esther is not merely a historical account; it is a timeless blueprint for living a life of purpose, faith, and action, reminding us of the potential within each of us to rise up and become agents of God's grace in our own time.

**"God hath not given us the spirit of fear; but of power, and of love, and of a sound mind."**

Esther's story transcends the historical context of ancient Persia; it resonates deeply with women's lives today, offering a potent message about the responsible use of influence. Her elevation to queen wasn't merely a matter of chance or beauty; it was a strategic positioning by a sovereign God, placing her in a position of unprecedented power and influence within a vast and complex empire. This wasn't merely a personal achievement but a divine setup designed to equip her to address a looming crisis that threatened her entire people.

The question then becomes, how did Esther leverage this position? How did she choose to use her influence? She didn't hoard her power, clinging to the privileges of her elevated status. Instead, she recognized the immense responsibility that came with it. Her influence, God-given and strategically placed, became a tool for justice, a weapon against oppression, and a lifeline for her people teetering on the brink of annihilation.

This resonates profoundly with the call on every woman's life to actively engage with the influence God has entrusted to her. Whether it's a position of leadership in a corporation, a platform in community service, or even the influence of a mother in her home, each woman wields a degree of power that can be used for either good or ill. Esther's example compels us to examine our own lives, scrutinizing the ways in which we exercise our influence.

Think of the women in your circle of influence – the mothers, sisters, daughters, friends, colleagues – and consider the ways their impact ripples outward. A mother's patient guidance shapes the character of her children, influencing their future choices and interactions with the world. A teacher's passion ignites a love for learning in her students, potentially shaping their career paths and lifelong interests. A business executive's ethical leadership sets the tone for her organization, impacting not just her employees but her customers and the wider community.

These seemingly small actions, these daily decisions, collectively form a powerful wave of influence, capable of shaping culture, impacting lives, and promoting positive change. This is the power Esther wielded, albeit on a grander scale. She used her influence not for personal gain but for the well-being of her people. Her actions weren't driven by ambition or self-interest but by a deep-seated love for her community and an unwavering faith in God's plan.

This principle transcends societal boundaries and professional roles. A woman's influence isn't limited to her workplace or her family. Her impact extends to every sphere of her life, from her local church to her volunteer work, to her casual conversations with friends and neighbors. Every interaction is an opportunity to sow seeds of kindness, compassion, and truth. Every decision is a statement, influencing the world around us, often in ways we don't immediately recognize.

The potential for positive influence is immeasurable. Consider the woman who advocates for fair wages in her workplace, standing up for the rights of her colleagues. Or the woman who volunteers at a local homeless shelter, offering hope and practical assistance to those in need. Or the woman who mentors young girls, empowering them to pursue their dreams and defy societal limitations. These seemingly ordinary acts are extraordinary expressions of influence, shaping the lives of others and contributing to a more just and compassionate world.

Esther's story challenges us to examine the areas where our influence may be dormant or misdirected. Are we using our talents and positions to champion justice and promote positive change? Are we actively seeking ways to amplify the voices of the marginalized and vulnerable? Are we boldly standing up against injustice and oppression, emulating Esther's courageous act of defying the powerful Haman? These questions force us to confront the realities of our own lives and the potential impact we could have if we choose to embrace our God-given influence fully.

It's crucial to recognize that wielding influence effectively isn't about seeking power for its own sake; it's about using the power we already possess to serve God and others. It's about using our gifts, talents, and resources to advance the kingdom of God on Earth. This requires intentionality, a deliberate choice to use our platforms for good, to speak truth to power, to champion the cause of the weak and the vulnerable.

The cultivation of a discerning heart is essential. We must learn to identify areas where our influence is most needed and where we can make the greatest impact. This requires prayer, seeking God's guidance, and a willingness to listen to the promptings of the Holy Spirit. It's about actively seeking opportunities to serve, to advocate, to stand up for what's right, even when it's difficult or unpopular.

Moreover, developing strong communication skills is essential for using our influence effectively. We must learn to articulate our message clearly and persuasively, to connect with people from diverse backgrounds, and to build bridges instead of walls. This involves active listening, empathy, and a willingness to understand different perspectives.

Beyond communication, building strong relationships is also crucial. Effective influence isn't wielded in isolation; it's built on trust, mutual respect, and shared values. Networking with like-minded individuals, forming strategic alliances, and building bridges of understanding are essential steps in amplifying our voice and extending our reach. Esther's success was partly due to her cultivated relationships within the Persian court, enabling her to navigate the complex political landscape and ultimately achieve her goal.

Furthermore, cultivating resilience is paramount. Using our influence for good often involves facing opposition, criticism, and even outright hostility. Esther's journey was fraught with danger, yet she persevered, driven by her faith and commitment to her people. We, too, must be prepared to face challenges, to withstand pressure, and to remain steadfast in our commitment to justice and positive change. The path to effective influence is rarely smooth or easy; it demands perseverance, courage, and unwavering faith.

## Strategy of Faith

The story of Esther is not just a historical account; it's a timeless parable illustrating the profound power of influence used for the betterment of humanity. It's a challenge to every woman, urging her to examine her own life, her own gifts, and the ways in which she can use her influence to impact the world around her. Let us each strive to be like Esther, using our God-given power not for personal gain but for the advancement of His kingdom, creating a ripple effect of positive change that transcends generations. Let us, like Esther, rise to the occasion and use our influence for good. The world needs our voices, our talents, our courage – it needs us to be agents of His grace and love in a world desperately in need of hope and redemption. The opportunities are abundant; let us seize them, empowered by faith and guided by the Holy Spirit.

Esther's story isn't just a tale of courage; it's a masterclass in strategic action born from faith. Her willingness to step out of her comfort zone, a zone of relative safety and privilege within the opulent Persian court, underscores a crucial truth for women today: true spiritual growth often requires us to venture beyond the familiar, to embrace the unknown with a heart full of faith and a spirit empowered by God.

Stepping out of your comfort zone isn't about reckless abandon; it's about calculated faith. It's about discerning God's leading and responding obediently, even when fear whispers doubts in your ear. For Esther, this meant approaching the king uninvited, a violation of court protocol that could have resulted in her immediate death. Yet, her obedience to Mordecai's urgent plea, driven by a deep faith in God's plan, propelled her into a moment of profound influence.

This act of stepping out resonates with the countless moments in our own lives where we're called to act in faith, even when logic screams otherwise. Consider the woman who leaves a secure job to pursue a calling in ministry despite the financial uncertainty. Or the mother who bravely advocates for her child's special needs in a system that feels indifferent. Or the young woman who speaks up against injustice in her community, facing potential backlash and ridicule. These are all instances of stepping out of comfort, driven by a conviction deeper than self-preservation.

The fear that grips us when faced with such choices is often rooted in the unknown. We fear failure, rejection, and the potential consequences of our actions. This fear is natural; it's a part of human experience. However, allowing fear to paralyze us and prevent us from pursuing God's calling is a betrayal of our potential and our faith. Esther's story reminds us that God often works through the unexpected, utilizing our seemingly small acts of obedience to bring about extraordinary outcomes.

Overcoming the fear of risk-taking requires a deliberate cultivation of faith. This involves nurturing a deep and personal relationship with God, spending time in prayer and scripture, allowing His word to permeate our hearts and minds. As we draw closer to God, our faith grows, and our fears diminish. The more we experience His faithfulness in the past, the more confident we become in His ability to guide us through the uncertainties of the future.

Furthermore, understanding God's character is crucial. He is not a distant, uncaring deity; He is a loving Father who desires our good and our flourishing. He doesn't call us to tasks beyond our abilities; He equips us with the strength and resources we need to succeed. Recognizing this truth helps alleviate the anxieties that often accompany stepping out of our comfort zones. We can approach challenging situations with greater confidence, knowing that God is with us every step of the way.

Surrounding ourselves with a supportive community is also essential. Sharing our fears and aspirations with trusted friends, family, or mentors can provide encouragement and accountability. These relationships can offer the emotional and spiritual support we need to persevere through challenging times. Having people who believe in us and offer words of affirmation and encouragement can make a significant difference in our ability to overcome fear and take risks for God's glory.

Practical steps toward stepping out include identifying areas where we feel the prompting of the Spirit of God. This might be a new ministry opportunity, a specific act of service, or a challenging conversation. Once we identify these areas, we need to start small, taking incremental steps forward. We don't need to leap from our comfort zone into the deep end all at once. Starting with small acts of faith can build our confidence and prepare us for greater challenges down the road.

Furthermore, celebrating small victories is crucial. Each time we step out of our comfort zone and experience success, even in small ways, we build our confidence and reinforce the belief that God is with us. These successes, no matter how insignificant they might seem, become building blocks for future endeavors, empowering us to take bigger risks and pursue more ambitious goals.

Esther's courageous act was not a one-time event; it was the culmination of a process of growth and spiritual maturity. It was a response to a divine calling, a recognition of her responsibility to her people, and a testament to her unwavering faith in God. Her example encourages us to step beyond our perceived limitations, to embrace the challenges and uncertainties that lie ahead, knowing that God is with us, equipping us with the strength and wisdom we need to succeed.

The journey of faith isn't always easy; it involves navigating doubt, facing opposition, and confronting our own fears. However, it's within these challenges that we truly grow, developing resilience, deepening our faith, and discovering the potential within us that God has placed there. Just as Esther's obedience led to the salvation of her people, our own acts of obedience, our willingness to step out of our comfort zones, can have far-reaching consequences, positively impacting our communities and advancing God's kingdom on Earth.

Stepping out of your comfort zone is an act of faith, an acknowledgment that God's plans for our lives are often greater than our own expectations. It's a journey of trust, a commitment to obedience, and a recognition of our potential to be agents of positive change in the world. Just as Esther's bravery saved countless lives, our own willingness to step out in faith can bring about immeasurable blessings and transformation, not just in our lives but in the lives of others. Let us embrace the challenge, step out, and discover the incredible things God has in store for us. Let us, like Esther, be instruments of His grace and love, impacting the world around us with faith, courage, and unwavering trust in His divine plan. The rewards far outweigh the risks; the blessings are immeasurable. Let us rise to the occasion, empowered by His love and guided by His grace.

## Discussion Questions

1. How does Esther's story differ from Hannah's in terms of the challenges each woman faces, and what are the key similarities in their expressions of faith?

2. In what ways does the book of Esther convey the theme of God's providence despite the absence of His name in the narrative?

3. What factors contributed to Esther's initial hesitation in approaching King Ahasuerus, and how does this reflect her understanding of faith and risk?

4. How does Esther's use of fasting and prayer illustrate the importance of spiritual preparation in critical moments?

5. In what ways does Esther's strategic approach to influencing the king demonstrate an active form of faith?

6. How does Esther's identity as a Jewish orphan affect her actions and decisions throughout the story?

7. What role does Mordecai play in shaping Esther's response to the crisis faced by the Jewish people?

8. How do Esther's actions during the banquets serve to highlight her intelligence and courage in the face of danger?

9. What does Esther's courage reveal about the nature of faith when faced with life-threatening situations?

10. How can Esther's story serve as a model for facing challenges in our own lives, particularly when it comes to balancing faith and strategy?

# CHAPTER 7

# MARY: HUMILITY AND OBEDIENCE

Unlike Esther's dramatic foray into the political arena, Mary's story unfolds in the quiet intimacy of a young woman's heart. Yet, the impact of her humble acceptance of God's will reverberates through centuries, shaping Christian theology and inspiring countless women to embrace their faith in the face of the extraordinary. Her story isn't one of daring exploits in the public eye but rather a testament to the profound power of inner strength, a quiet obedience born from a deeply rooted faith.

The narrative in Luke 1 presents Mary not as a queen or a warrior, but as a young, unassuming woman, betrothed but not yet married. This context is crucial. In a society governed by strict social hierarchies and religious laws, Mary's position held little power or influence. She was not a princess destined for greatness, nor a prophetess accustomed to divine pronouncements. She was, quite simply, an ordinary young woman, living an ordinary life in anticipation of an ordinary future.

Then came the angel Gabriel, a messenger of the Most High, bearing news that shattered the ordinary. His announcement wasn't a gentle suggestion; it was a divine decree, a command that would forever alter the course of human history: "You will conceive and give birth to a son, and you are to give him the name Jesus." (Luke 1:31). Imagine the weight of that statement, the sheer enormity of the request, cascading upon a young woman who likely lived a life characterized by routine and expectation. To be chosen to carry the Son of God, the Messiah, the long-awaited King of Israel, was a responsibility beyond comprehension.

The angel's message wasn't simply about the birth of a child; it was about the fulfillment of God's ancient promises, the dawn of a new era in salvation history. Mary's response, therefore, isn't just a personal acceptance of an unusual pregnancy, but an embrace of God's cosmic plan for redemption. Her "yes" was not a casual affirmation but a profound act of faith, a surrender to a destiny far greater than anything she could have ever imagined for herself.

Mary's immediate response reveals the depth of her faith and her profound humility. She doesn't demand proof, question the messenger's credentials, or bargain with God for a more comfortable outcome. Instead, she articulates a question born not of skepticism but of awe-filled wonder: "How can this be? I am a virgin." (Luke 1:34). This isn't a rejection, but a genuine inquiry, an expression of humble acknowledgment of her own limitations and humanity in the face of the divine. It's a question that reveals a spirit open to the supernatural, receptive to the unimaginable work of God.

Her subsequent response is even more revealing of her character. She doesn't seize upon this extraordinary event as an opportunity for personal aggrandizement, or a chance to leverage power and influence. Instead, she submits wholeheartedly to God's will: "I am the Lord's servant. May your word to me be fulfilled." (Luke 1:38).

This simple declaration, filled with both humility and unwavering obedience, underscores the essence of Mary's character. She recognizes herself as a servant, a vessel chosen by God to fulfill His purpose, not a participant in shaping that purpose.

This act of humble submission is crucial for understanding Mary's role and the message of her story. It refutes the notion that God only chooses those who are powerful, influential, or already successful. Mary's story proclaims that God often chooses the humble, the seemingly insignificant, to accomplish His greatest works. Her willingness to submit to God's will, despite the personal sacrifices and potential social consequences, stands as a powerful example for women across generations.

Consider the social implications of her situation. A pregnancy outside of marriage in her cultural context could have led to disgrace, rejection, and even death by stoning. Yet, Mary's faith transcended the fear of social stigma. Her obedience to God overshadowed any personal concerns or anxieties about her reputation or future. This highlights the transformative power of faith: it empowers us to overcome fear and embrace uncertainty, confident in God's unwavering love and protection.

Mary's humility isn't passive resignation but active engagement with God's plan. It's a willingness to surrender her personal desires and ambitions to the divine will, trusting that God will provide the necessary strength and guidance. Her journey wasn't easy. She likely faced moments of doubt, fear, and uncertainty, yet her unwavering faith in God's goodness and faithfulness sustained her throughout the ordeal.

Mary's example encourages us to examine our own responses to God's call in our lives. Do we readily embrace His will, or do we hesitate, bargain, or attempt to control the outcome? Are we willing to submit to His plan, even when it requires significant personal sacrifice? Mary's life teaches us that true humility isn't about self-deprecation or self-effacement but about recognizing our dependence on God and surrendering our will to His.

The parallels between Mary's experience and the challenges faced by women today are striking. Many women grapple with societal expectations, cultural norms, and personal limitations that can restrict their spiritual growth and potential. Mary's story offers a powerful counter-narrative, demonstrating that God's call transcends social expectations and cultural constraints. He calls women from all walks of life, in all circumstances, to partner with Him in His work in the world.

Furthermore, Mary's humility teaches us about the importance of selfless service. Her willingness to become the mother of Jesus wasn't about personal glory or recognition but about fulfilling God's purpose for the salvation of humanity. Her life was a ministry of service, a life dedicated to nurturing and supporting her son, the Messiah. Her humility serves as a model for Christian women today, encouraging them to prioritize service over self-promotion, to seek God's glory rather than personal gain.

In a world that often values ambition, achievement, and personal recognition, Mary's humility stands as a refreshing counterpoint. It reminds us that true fulfillment is not found in worldly success, but in humbly serving God and His people. Her life teaches us that the most significant achievements are often accomplished not through power or influence, but through quiet obedience and selfless service.

### Humble Acceptance and Intentional Faith

Mary's humble acceptance of God's will was not a one-time event, but a defining characteristic of her life. It shaped her responses to various challenges, guided her choices, and fueled her unwavering devotion to God. Her life was a living embodiment of faith, humility, and obedience, providing a powerful example for women striving to live lives pleasing to God.

Consider the Magnificat, Mary's song of praise recorded in Luke 1:46-55. This song isn't a boastful proclamation of her own importance but a humble expression of gratitude to God for His mercy and faithfulness. She sings of God's power to uplift the humble and cast down the mighty, highlighting His preference for the meek and the marginalized. Her song reflects the very essence of her character: humility, gratitude, and unwavering trust in God's plan.

The life of Mary, therefore, isn't a static historical account but a dynamic narrative with enduring relevance for women today. It's a story of faith, humility, and obedience that empowers women to embrace their spiritual potential and live lives of purpose and meaning. Her example challenges us to examine our own hearts, to assess our willingness to submit to God's will, and to embrace the transformative power of humble obedience. Her "yes" echoes through the ages, urging us to answer God's call with the same faith, humility, and unwavering trust that characterized the life of the mother of Jesus. It is a "yes" that changed the world, and a "yes" that continues to inspire women to step into their God-given purpose with grace, courage, and unwavering faith. It is a "yes" that reminds us that even in the quiet corners of our lives, even in our seemingly insignificant moments, God can work mightily through us if we will only surrender to His will, embracing our role as His humble servants.

Mary's willingness to surrender to God's plan wasn't a passive acceptance; it was an active choice, a daily commitment to aligning her will with His. It wasn't the absence of struggle, but rather a consistent choice to trust in His sovereignty even amidst the uncertainties and anxieties inherent in her extraordinary circumstances. This active surrender is a crucial element for women seeking to fulfill their God-given purpose in today's complex world. It demands a conscious effort to relinquish control, to let go of our own ambitions and agendas, and to embrace the unknown with faith.

Consider the practical implications of this surrender. It means being open to unexpected opportunities, even those that may initially seem daunting or uncomfortable. It requires a willingness to step outside our comfort zones, to venture into uncharted territory, trusting that God will guide our paths and equip us for the challenges ahead. For Mary, this meant embracing a pregnancy that defied societal norms and risked social ostracism. For us, it might mean accepting a new job, moving to a different city, or embarking on a ministry that stretches us beyond our perceived capabilities.

The key is to cultivate a heart posture of dependence on God. This isn't a sign of weakness but rather a recognition of our inherent limitations and our utter reliance on God's grace and strength. It involves actively seeking His guidance through prayer, scripture study, and fellowship with other believers. It means learning to discern His voice amidst the noise of our own anxieties and the distractions of the world. It is a process of actively listening for God's guidance and discerning His will through prayer, scripture, and community. It's about learning to trust His timing, wisdom, and love, even when we don't understand the path He is leading us on.

Surrendering to God's plan doesn't mean passively accepting whatever happens; it means actively partnering with Him in the unfolding of His purposes. It's about seeking His will and cooperating with His work in our lives. It's not about resigning ourselves to fate, but about actively participating in God's redemptive story. This active collaboration requires faith, courage, and a willingness to trust God even when the path is unclear.

This active surrender requires a daily, intentional act of faith. It's not a one-time decision, but a continual process of aligning our hearts and minds with God's will. It involves consciously choosing to trust Him, even when faced with doubts, fears, and uncertainties. It is about constantly seeking God's leading, discerning his voice, and obediently following where he leads.

Mary's journey wasn't without its challenges. She faced social stigma, potential rejection, and the daunting responsibility of bearing the Son of God. Yet, her unwavering trust in God's goodness and faithfulness sustained her throughout the ordeal. Her story is a testament to the transformative power of faith—a faith that enables us to overcome fear, embrace uncertainty, and find strength in the midst of adversity.

Her story also reminds us that surrendering to God's plan often requires us to let go of our own expectations and desires. We may have meticulously crafted plans for our lives, carefully mapped out our career paths, and envisioned a specific future for ourselves. But God's plan may be vastly different, leading us in unexpected directions and challenging us to step beyond our comfort zones.

This surrendering is not about self-abnegation or denying our passions and talents. It is about recognizing that God's plan for our lives is far grander and more fulfilling than anything we could ever imagine for ourselves. It's about allowing God to use our unique gifts and abilities to accomplish His purposes in ways we might never have conceived. It's about aligning our desires with His, allowing Him to shape and refine our ambitions.

Surrendering to God's plan is an act of faith, an affirmation that He knows our paths better than we do and that His plans for us are ultimately good and beneficial. This isn't blind faith; it's a faith informed by Scripture, prayer, and the guidance of the Holy Ghost.

How, then, do we practically surrender to God's plan? It begins with prayer, seeking God's guidance through consistent communication with Him. It involves studying Scripture, allowing God's word to illuminate our paths and shape our perspectives. It also includes seeking wisdom and counsel from trusted mentors and spiritual leaders. It means being actively involved in a community of faith and seeking support and encouragement from other believers.

Furthermore, it requires a willingness to listen to the still, small voice of God, discerning His guidance in the everyday details of our lives. This may involve a moment of profound clarity or a gradual unfolding of God's will as we journey along His path. It's about cultivating sensitivity to God's leading, being attentive to His promptings, and obediently responding to His call.

Surrendering also involves releasing our anxieties and fears to God. It's acknowledging our limitations and trusting in His infinite power and provision. It's choosing to trust that He will work all things together for our good, even when we don't see the immediate benefits or understand His purposes. This releases us from the burden of trying to control every aspect of our lives, allowing God to orchestrate His plan in His own time and in His own way.

Finally, surrendering to God's plan involves embracing uncertainty. It's acknowledging that we don't have all the answers and trusting that He does. It's choosing to step forward in faith, even when the path ahead is unclear, knowing He will guide our steps and provide for our needs. It's a leap of faith, a trust in God's unwavering love and faithfulness.

## A Powerful Example

Mary's story provides a powerful example for us today. She stands as a beacon of faith, humility, and obedience, demonstrating the transformative power of surrendering to God's plan. Her "yes" resonates through the ages, inspiring women to embrace their God-given purpose and to trust in His sovereign will, even amidst the uncertainties and challenges of life. Her example encourages us to let go of our self-reliance, to embrace our dependence on God, and to walk confidently in His path, knowing that He is leading us to a future far greater than anything we could have imagined. It's a future filled with His grace, His love, and His abundant blessings. It's a future where we can truly discover and fulfill our God-given destiny, becoming powerful warriors of faith, ready to embrace whatever challenges lie ahead. This is the essence of surrendering—a heart posture of obedience, a commitment to partnership with God, and a trust in His unwavering love and provision. It's a journey, not a destination, a continual process of aligning our will with His, seeking His guidance, and embracing His plan for our lives.

Mary's story, so often recounted in hushed reverence, is more than a narrative of a miraculous conception; it's a potent testament to unwavering faith in the face of the utterly unknown. The angel Gabriel's announcement wasn't a gentle whisper of pleasant news; it was a seismic shift, an upheaval of her carefully constructed life, a challenge that defied logic and societal expectations. Imagine the sheer audacity of the request: to bear the Son of God, a task fraught with peril, both physical and spiritual. The weight of this revelation must have been immense, crushing even the most devout heart. Yet, Mary's response, a humble "yes," echoes through the centuries, a beacon of unwavering trust in the divine plan, even when veiled in profound mystery.

This "yes" wasn't a naive acceptance of the inexplicable; it was a conscious choice born from a deep-seated faith, a faith nurtured through prayer, scripture, and a life lived in close communion with God. It was a decision made not in the comfort of certainty but in the crucible of uncertainty, a testament to the power of faith to illuminate even the darkest corners of the unknown. To fully appreciate the magnitude of Mary's faith, we must consider the socio-cultural context of her time. A young, unmarried woman pregnant, in a society governed by strict religious and social codes, faced profound ostracism and potential ruin. The societal ramifications were far-reaching; her reputation, her standing in the community, and her very future were all jeopardized. This wasn't simply a matter of personal inconvenience; it was a life-altering event with potentially devastating consequences.

Yet, amidst this storm of uncertainty, Mary's faith remained steadfast. She didn't demand answers or explanations; she didn't bargain with God or try to control the outcome. She didn't question the divine plan, even though it was completely outside her understanding. Her faith wasn't blind; it was an informed trust based on her relationship with God, a relationship honed through years of spiritual discipline and devotion. This active trust is crucial for us today as we navigate our own uncertain paths. We, too, face moments when the future is shrouded in ambiguity, when the path ahead is unclear, when fear and anxiety threaten to overwhelm us.

Mary's response is a powerful example of how we can cultivate unwavering faith amidst life's uncertainties. It is not a passive acceptance of whatever may come but an active engagement with God, a continuous seeking of His will, a resolute trust in His sovereign plan, even when that plan is hidden from our view. This active engagement involves several key aspects.

Firstly, it requires a commitment to prayer, consistent communication with God, pouring out our hearts to Him, seeking His guidance, and listening for His still, small voice. This isn't a one-time prayer, a desperate plea in moments of crisis; it's a sustained dialogue, a continuous conversation with the divine. It's about cultivating a deep personal connection with God, a relationship built on trust, intimacy, and unwavering faith.

Secondly, it necessitates diligent study of scripture. The word of God is a lamp unto our feet and a light unto our path, illuminating the darkness and guiding our steps. Through scripture, we learn about God's character, His faithfulness, His love, and His power. We see how He has worked in the lives of others, how He has guided them through trials and tribulations, and how He has ultimately brought them through to victory. Mary's deep understanding of scripture likely provided her with the spiritual foundation to accept her extraordinary calling, an understanding that reinforced her faith and enabled her to embrace the unknown.

Thirdly, seeking guidance from spiritual mentors and trusted advisors is essential. Surrounding ourselves with a supportive faith community can provide strength, encouragement, and perspective when faced with uncertainty. Mary's journey was likely supported by her close relationship with Elizabeth, whose own miraculous pregnancy offered solace and confirmation of God's work. This human connection, this support system, strengthened her faith and helped her navigate the challenges ahead.

Furthermore, cultivating a spirit of humility is crucial. Mary's willingness to surrender to God's plan wasn't rooted in arrogance or self-reliance; it stemmed from a deep sense of humility, a recognition of her own limitations, and a profound trust in God's omnipotence. This humility wasn't a passive resignation; it was an active choice to relinquish control, step aside, and allow God to work in her life. This is a constant struggle for all of us. Our pride often whispers that we have a better plan and that we know what is best for our lives. Mary's example reminds us that true strength lies not in self-sufficiency but in our humble reliance upon God.

Finally, embracing the unknown with courage is paramount. Mary's journey wasn't paved with certainty; it was a path shrouded in mystery, a trek into uncharted territory. Yet, she walked forward with faith, trusting that God would guide her steps, provide for her needs, and ultimately bring her through to victory. This requires a willingness to step outside of our comfort zones and to venture into places where we feel insecure or vulnerable. It calls for courage, for a steadfast belief that even in the midst of uncertainty, God is with us, guiding and protecting us, leading us to a future that surpasses our wildest dreams.

Therefore, Mary's faith wasn't a passive acceptance of fate; it was an active partnership with God, a dance of surrender and trust, obedience and unwavering faith. Her "yes" wasn't a simple affirmation; it was a declaration of her complete trust in God's plan, a commitment to follow His leading, even when that leading led her into the heart of the unknown. Her life stands as a powerful example for us today, urging us to embrace uncertainty with courage, to cultivate a deeper relationship with God through prayer and scripture study, to seek support from our community of faith, and to humbly surrender to His divine plan.

For it is in the surrender, in the letting go of our own control, that we truly discover the boundless grace and transformative power of God. It is in the embracing of the unknown, in the trusting heart of faith, that we discover the profound and fulfilling life God has planned for us. And like Mary, we can find strength, peace, and unwavering hope amidst life's greatest challenges.

This is the legacy of Mary, a timeless lesson in faith, humility, and the courageous embrace of the unknown. It is a journey of trust, a path paved with both joy and uncertainty, a testament to God's unwavering love and grace. This is the journey of faith, a journey that awaits each one of us, a journey to a life beyond our wildest dreams.

## Discussion Questions

1. How does Mary's story differ from Esther's in terms of their roles and the impact they have on their respective narratives?

2. What significance does the context of Mary's life hold in understanding her response to the angel Gabriel?

3. How does the announcement of Jesus' birth by Gabriel represent a shift in salvation history?

4. In what ways does Mary's question, "How can this be?" reflect her character and faith?

5. What can we learn from Mary's immediate acceptance of her role as the Lord's servant?

6. How does Mary's humility and obedience challenge the notion that God only chooses the powerful or influential?

7. What are the potential social consequences Mary faced as a result of her pregnancy, and how did her faith help her overcome these fears?

8. How does Mary's example encourage us to reflect on our own willingness to submit to God's will in our lives?

9. In what ways can we actively engage with God's plan, similar to how Mary did, rather than resigning ourselves to it?

10. How does the concept of true humility in Mary's story differ from common perceptions of humility in today's society?

# CHAPTER 8

# DISCOVERING YOUR SPIRITUAL GIFTS

Having explored the profound example of Mary's obedience and the journey of discerning God's call, we now turn our attention inward, to the unique talents and spiritual gifts God has bestowed upon each of us. Just as Mary possessed a unique blend of faith, humility, and courage, each woman possesses a unique spiritual profile, a constellation of gifts designed to serve God's purposes in the world. Understanding and embracing these gifts is crucial to fulfilling our individual destinies and contributing meaningfully to the body of Christ. Recognizing these gifts isn't about self-aggrandizement; it's about discerning how God has uniquely equipped us to serve Him and His people.

The Bible speaks extensively about spiritual gifts, describing them as manifestations of the Holy Ghost's power working through believers (1 Corinthians 12). These gifts aren't merely talents or abilities; they are divinely bestowed graces, empowered by the Spirit, enabling us to serve others and build up the church. They are diverse, reflecting the multifaceted nature of God's love and the varied needs of His people. Some gifts are more outwardly focused, such as teaching, preaching, or prophecy, while others are more inwardly focused, such as discernment, mercy, or encouragement. Regardless of their expression, each gift is essential to the health and growth of the body of Christ.

Identifying your unique talents requires introspection, prayer, and a willingness to honestly assess your strengths and weaknesses. It's a process of self-discovery, guided by the Spirit, leading to a deeper understanding of your God-given potential. It's not about comparing yourself to others; it's about recognizing your unique contribution to the tapestry of God's work. Start by considering your natural inclinations, those activities that come easily to you, that you find yourself drawn to, and that you excel at. These innate abilities often serve as a foundation for developing your spiritual gifts. For example, if you have a natural aptitude for writing, you may discover a gift for teaching or writing devotional materials. If you have a deep empathy for others, you may find yourself gifted in counseling or providing pastoral care.

Next, reflect on areas where you have experienced God's presence and power in your life. Have you been unexpectedly empowered to comfort someone in grief? Have you found yourself naturally leading a group or team? Have you experienced a sense of deep spiritual insight or understanding in a particular area? These instances often highlight areas of spiritual gifting. Think back to specific situations where you felt a particular sense of fulfillment or purpose. This feeling of divine empowerment is often a clear indication of where your gifts lie. Journaling can be a valuable tool in this process, allowing you to record your thoughts and reflections, track patterns, and discern recurring themes.

Prayer is essential in this process of self-discovery. Ask God to reveal your spiritual gifts to you. Ask Him to open your eyes to your talents and how you can best use them for His glory. This is not a passive request; it requires an active posture of seeking, listening, and responding to the Spirit's guidance. Spend time in quiet contemplation, allowing God to illuminate your heart and mind. Read scripture, paying attention to passages that speak about spiritual gifts. Meditate on these verses, allowing God's Word to shape your understanding and perspective. Consider the gifts mentioned in 1 Corinthians 12 and Romans 12, pondering which ones resonate with your heart and experience. Remember, God's gifts are given for the benefit of others, not for personal gain or recognition.

Another valuable tool is seeking feedback from trusted mentors or spiritual advisors. These individuals, who know you well and deeply understand spiritual gifts, can offer valuable insights and perspectives. Share your reflections and experiences with them, asking for their prayers and discernment. Their insights can help you to identify patterns and clarify your understanding of your gifts. Don't be afraid to solicit feedback; a well-meaning mentor can highlight things you may not see in yourself. They can provide objective observations that can aid in your self-assessment. This isn't about seeking validation; it's about seeking wisdom and guidance from those who have a broader perspective.

In addition to seeking feedback from others, participate actively in your church or ministry. Try different roles and responsibilities, testing your abilities and discovering where you feel most fulfilled. Volunteer in areas that seem intriguing, even if you are hesitant or unsure of your abilities. These experiences provide valuable opportunities for growth and discernment. God often reveals our gifts through the process of serving others. We may discover hidden talents or previously unrecognized strengths. Embrace opportunities for service as a path to discovering your potential. Remember, spiritual gifts are meant to be used, not stored away.

Beyond your church or ministry, look to areas of passion in your life. What do you find yourself gravitating toward? What brings you joy and satisfaction? These passions often align with your spiritual gifts. The activities that energize and uplift you can be valuable indicators of your God-given abilities. If you find yourself repeatedly drawn to certain activities or causes, explore whether these passions could be channeled into ministry or service. Remember, your gifts are not limited to formal church settings; they can be employed in all aspects of your life.

Once you have identified some potential areas of giftedness, don't feel pressured to confine yourself to a single gift. Most individuals possess multiple spiritual gifts, working together in unique combinations. It's rare that a person only possesses one gift, and even rarer that one gift is sufficient to fulfill one's calling. Embrace the diversity of your talents, recognizing that each contributes to your overall purpose and ministry. As you serve and grow, you may discover new gifts or a deepening understanding of those you already possess. This is a continual process of revelation and development.

Identifying your spiritual gifts isn't a one-time event; it's a journey of ongoing discovery and refinement. It's a process that requires continual prayer, self-reflection, and engagement in ministry. Remember, God's gifts are not meant to be kept hidden; they are meant to be shared with the world. You will experience a profound sense of purpose, fulfillment, and connection with God as you embrace your unique abilities and use them to serve others. Your gifts become channels through which God's love and grace flow into the lives of others, transforming lives and building His kingdom. It is in this surrender, in this active participation in God's work, that you truly discover the depth and breadth of your spiritual potential, becoming the mighty warrior woman God created you to be. Let your light shine brightly, reflecting the glory of God in all that you do.

## Spiritual Discipline

Having identified potential areas of spiritual giftedness, the next crucial step is cultivating and developing those gifts through consistent spiritual disciplines. These aren't merely optional add-ons to our lives; they are essential practices that nurture our relationship with God, deepen our understanding of His Word, and empower us to effectively utilize the gifts He has bestowed upon us. Think of spiritual disciplines as the fertile soil in which our spiritual gifts can flourish. Even the most promising gifts can remain dormant or underdeveloped without consistent nurturing.

Prayer, perhaps the most fundamental spiritual discipline, is the cornerstone of our relationship with God. It is through prayer that we communicate with the Divine, seeking His guidance, wisdom, and strength. In the context of developing our spiritual gifts, prayer is not simply a request list but a deep communion of heart and spirit. We must cultivate a consistent prayer life, setting aside dedicated time each day for focused prayer. This could involve morning or evening prayers or perhaps shorter periods of prayer throughout the day. The key is regularity and intentionality.

Beyond general prayers of thanksgiving and petition, we should engage in specific prayers related to our spiritual gifts. Ask God to reveal how He wants to use your gifts. Ask for wisdom in discerning opportunities to serve. Ask for strength to overcome any obstacles or fears that may hinder using your gifts. Pray for the people you will serve, asking God to bless them and to open their hearts to receive your ministry. Prayer doesn't just prepare us for service; it makes us more sensitive to the promptings of God, guiding us toward specific areas where our gifts are needed. Intercessory prayer for others often strengthens one's own gifts of empathy and compassion.

Bible study is another crucial spiritual discipline. Through the study of God's Word, we gain a deeper understanding of His character, His will, and His purposes for our lives. Regular Bible study equips us to discern truth from falsehood, to understand biblical principles, and to apply them to our lives and ministries. For those with gifts of teaching or preaching, Bible study is essential for preparing effective and biblically sound messages. For those with prophetic gifts, it helps them to discern the voice of God and to interpret His messages accurately. Even if your gifts aren't directly related to teaching, a consistent scripture study fosters spiritual maturity, enriching your entire life and ministry.

Effective Bible study goes beyond simply reading through the scriptures. It requires careful consideration, meditation, and application. Consider using various Bible study methods, such as journaling, memorization, and group study. Different approaches will appeal to different learning styles and personalities. Employing various methods allows you to not only grasp the text but also to process and apply its meaning on a deeper level. For example, incorporating art or music into your Bible study can enhance your understanding and retention if you're drawn to creative expression. Likewise, using study Bibles or commentaries can deepen your insight. The most important aspect is to make it a consistent, meaningful engagement.

Fellowship with other believers is another essential spiritual discipline. The church is the body of Christ, and we are called to be active and contributing members. Through fellowship, we receive encouragement, support, and accountability. We learn from each other's strengths and experiences, and we are challenged to grow in our faith. Fellowship provides a safe space to share our gifts, receive feedback, and grow in spiritual maturity. The support of fellow believers can be invaluable as we navigate the challenges of using our gifts. Engaging in community allows us to be equipped and sharpened.

Active participation in church or ministry activities is a direct application of fellowship. It allows us to practice our gifts, serve others, and experience the joy of using our abilities for God's glory. This could involve teaching a Sunday school class, leading a small group, serving on a church committee, or volunteering in a community outreach program. Stepping outside our comfort zones often leads to the most significant growth, revealing latent strengths and encouraging us to further develop our talents. Even small acts of service, such as assisting with hospitality or administrative tasks, can nurture our spiritual growth and enhance our gifts. Through serving, we become more aware of our strengths and weaknesses.

Beyond these core disciplines, consider incorporating practices like fasting, journaling, and solitude. While sometimes misunderstood, fasting is a powerful spiritual discipline that allows us to focus on God and deepen our dependence on Him. It can enhance prayer and provide a deeper connection with the Divine. Journaling provides a means of reflecting on our spiritual experiences and insights, allowing us to track our growth and identify areas where God is working in our lives. Solitude, the intentional setting aside time for quiet reflection and communion with God, cultivates spiritual awareness and fosters a deeper relationship with the Divine. These practices should be incorporated deliberately, according to one's personal preferences and the leading of the Holy Ghost.

Developing spiritual disciplines is not a one-time event but a lifelong journey. It's a consistent process of growth and refinement, requiring commitment and perseverance. There will be times when our spiritual disciplines feel challenging, and we may be tempted to neglect them. During these times, it is crucial to rely on the grace and strength that God provides. Remembering our motivations for pursuing these disciplines, particularly their impact on our spiritual gifts, can help us to remain steadfast in our commitment.

## Nurture Your Spiritual Life

The key is to find a rhythm that works for you. It's not about rigidly adhering to a prescribed schedule; it's about consistently nurturing your spiritual life. Be flexible, adjusting your practices as needed to accommodate life's changing demands. The goal is not to perfectly adhere to a regimen but to cultivate a genuine, intimate relationship with God that empowers you to use your gifts for His glory. Through consistent engagement in these spiritual disciplines, we become more attuned to God and more effective in utilizing our gifts to serve Him and others. Remember that these disciplines are not just about personal growth, but also about preparing ourselves to be effective vessels through which God can work His transformative power in the lives of those around us. It's in this ongoing process of refining and nurturing our spiritual lives that we truly unlock the immense potential God has placed within us. Our spiritual disciplines ultimately become the catalyst for fulfilling our unique callings and becoming the mighty warrior women God intends us to be.

Having cultivated a strong foundation in spiritual disciplines, we now turn our attention to the practical application of our spiritual gifts: serving others. This isn't merely an optional activity; it's the very essence of Christian discipleship. As we grow in our understanding of God's love and grace, we are compelled to share that love and grace with the world around us. Our spiritual gifts, uniquely bestowed by God, become the tools through which we extend God's kingdom and build up His church.

The Bible is replete with examples of selfless service. Jesus, the ultimate model, dedicated his life to serving others, culminating in His sacrificial death on the cross. His ministry was characterized by compassion, healing, and teaching. Throughout scripture, we see countless individuals utilizing their God-given gifts to meet the needs of those around them. Consider the apostle Paul, whose tireless missionary journeys and prolific writings transformed the early church. His gift of teaching, coupled with his unwavering faith, shaped the course of Christianity for centuries to come. Or consider Dorcas, praised for her numerous acts of charity (Acts 9:36-42). Her life exemplified the power of using practical skills to serve those in need. These examples serve as powerful reminders that our gifts are not meant to be hoarded but shared generously.

Serving others through our spiritual gifts is not about personal gain or recognition. It's about humbly using our abilities to uplift, encourage, and bless others, reflecting God's love in tangible ways. This kind of service transcends cultural norms and expectations, emphasizing a selfless devotion to the needs of those around us. It's about seeing Christ in others and ministering to them as we would minister to Him.

The ways in which we can serve others through our spiritual gifts are as diverse as the gifts themselves. Those with the gift of teaching can impart biblical knowledge and wisdom through Sunday school classes, Bible studies, or mentoring relationships. They can craft compelling sermons or write insightful articles that nurture the faith of others. Those with the gift of prophecy can offer words of encouragement, guidance, or warning, helping others discern God's will for their lives. Their words should always be rooted in scripture and motivated by love and compassion.

Those gifted in administration can effectively organize and manage church programs, ensuring that the various ministries function smoothly and efficiently. They provide the necessary logistical support that allows other ministries to flourish. Individuals blessed with a gift of hospitality can create a welcoming and nurturing environment within the church community, making others feel valued and cherished. This involves more than just welcoming people at the church door; it's about extending kindness and understanding to everyone you encounter.

Those with a gift of mercy and compassion can offer practical assistance to those in need, visit the sick, provide for the poor, or offer emotional support to those struggling. This involves actively listening to their concerns, offering prayers of comfort, and providing tangible help whenever possible. This practical demonstration of God's love often has a profound impact on others.

The gift of helping often manifests in practical skills like organizing events, offering technical support, or providing administrative assistance. These might seem like smaller gifts, but they are crucial to the smooth operation of a church or ministry. This gift allows those with different spiritual gifts to flourish by providing a solid infrastructure for their ministries.

Those with the gift of evangelism can share the good news of Jesus Christ with others, boldly proclaiming the message of salvation and inviting them into a relationship with God. They might be equipped to engage in deep Biblical conversations or might be better suited to simply sharing their personal testimony of faith. Each approach is valuable in God's kingdom.

The opportunities for service are endless. Consider volunteering at a homeless shelter, visiting the elderly in nursing homes, mentoring at-risk youth, or participating in international mission trips. These acts of service not only benefit those we serve, but they also deepen our own relationship with God. As we pour ourselves out for others, we discover a greater capacity for empathy, compassion, and love. We find that by giving, we receive far more in return.

However, serving others effectively requires self-awareness. We must accurately assess our own strengths and weaknesses to identify the areas where our gifts can best be utilized. It also demands humility, recognizing that our gifts are not our own, but a gracious bestowal from God. We must always be willing to serve in obscurity, seeking God's glory above personal recognition. The most impactful service is often done quietly and without fanfare.

Identifying your gifts is the first step, but consistently applying them requires discipline and perseverance. There will be times when we feel discouraged or overwhelmed, but we must remember that God is our strength and our guide. He will equip us for the tasks He sets before us and provide the support we need to persevere. Prayer, both for ourselves and for those we serve, becomes crucial as we navigate the challenges of ministry.

Furthermore, seeking mentorship and guidance from experienced Christians can be incredibly beneficial. Learning from those who have successfully used their spiritual gifts can help us avoid common pitfalls and develop a more effective approach to service. Through this mentorship, we find ourselves strengthened, challenged, and guided towards fulfilling our full potential in ministry. The wisdom and experience of others can often be invaluable in our growth.

Finally, remember the importance of maintaining a balance in our lives. Serving others should not consume us to the point of burnout. We must prioritize our own spiritual well-being, ensuring that we are consistently replenishing ourselves through prayer, Bible study, and fellowship. Only then can we effectively serve others without compromising our own health and stability. This balance is vital for sustaining a long-term commitment to ministry and avoiding the pitfalls of exhaustion or spiritual depletion. Maintaining a healthy relationship with God, ourselves, and our community is essential for continued effectiveness in serving others. In this all-inclusive approach, we truly discover the profound joy and fulfillment that comes from using our gifts to build up God's kingdom. The journey of discovering and utilizing our spiritual gifts is a lifelong process of learning, growing, and serving—a journey that leads to both personal transformation and a profound impact on the lives of those around us.

**"As each has received a gift, use it to serve one another, as good stewards of God's varied grace" (1 Peter 4:1)**

Many women, even after identifying their spiritual gifts, hesitate to use them. A deep-seated fear often holds them back, whispering doubts and anxieties that can be paralyzing. This fear manifests in various ways: fear of failure, fear of judgment, fear of rejection, fear of inadequacy, or even fear of success. These fears, often rooted in past experiences or ingrained societal expectations, can effectively silence the powerful voice of God calling us to action. Understanding the root of these fears is the first step toward overcoming them.

Fear of failure is perhaps the most common obstacle. We may worry about making mistakes, embarrassing ourselves, or not measuring up to others' expectations. We may envision the worst-case scenario, imagining negative reactions or criticism. This fear can be especially potent in ministry contexts, where the stakes feel high, and the consequences of perceived failure can seem significant. Yet, it's important to remember that God does not expect perfection. He values our willingness to serve and our commitment to His work, even amidst our imperfections. He works through our flaws, using our vulnerabilities to demonstrate His grace and power. Our failures are not the end of our ministry; they are opportunities for growth, learning, and a deeper dependence on God. The Apostle Paul, in his letter to the Corinthians, reminds us that "we have this treasure in jars of clay to show that this all-surpassing power is from God and not from us" (2 Corinthians 4:7). Our frailty underscores the divine power at work.

Fear of judgment is closely related to fear of failure. We may worry about what others will think of us, whether they will approve of our actions or whether they will criticize our efforts. This fear can stem from past experiences of rejection or criticism or from a pervasive sense of insecurity. We may worry about being judged by our peers, our church leaders, or even our families. However, we must remember that our ultimate judge is God, and His judgment is one of love and grace. He sees our hearts and our intentions, and He values our obedience above our perfection. While the opinions of others matter, our primary focus must remain on pleasing God, not seeking human approval. The approval of God transcends any earthly judgment.

The fear of rejection can be particularly devastating for women in ministry. Society has often relegated women to secondary roles, fostering an environment where they may feel unwelcome or undervalued. This can lead to a deep-seated fear of being rejected or marginalized if they step into leadership roles or openly express their gifts. However, we are called to overcome this fear by embracing our identity in Christ. We are daughters of the King, uniquely created and loved by God, possessing inherent worth and value. No earthly rejection can diminish the love and acceptance we have found in Him. The rejection of others cannot overshadow the unwavering embrace of our heavenly Father.

Furthermore, the fear of inadequacy often plagues women who are hesitant to use their spiritual gifts. We may compare ourselves to others, perceiving their talents as superior to our own. We may doubt our abilities, questioning whether we are qualified or capable of fulfilling God's calling. Yet, it's crucial to remember that God works through our weaknesses, not just our strengths. He calls us to use the gifts He has given us, not to compare ourselves with the gifts of others. Each of us has unique talents and abilities, perfectly suited to the specific tasks He has prepared for us.

Finally, even the fear of success can hinder the use of our spiritual gifts. We may worry about the responsibilities and challenges that come with success. We may fear that success will change us or distance us from God. However, success in God's kingdom is not about personal advancement or worldly recognition. It's about fulfilling His purpose, impacting His kingdom, and glorifying His name. True success lies in our faithfulness and obedience, not in outward achievements. If we are blessed with opportunities for greater service, it's an indication of God's trust in our abilities and an invitation to use them to build His kingdom.

Overcoming these fears is not a passive process; it requires conscious effort and steadfast faith. Here are some practical strategies for overcoming the fear of using your spiritual gifts:

**Prayer:** Consistent prayer is essential. Pray for courage, wisdom, and strength. Ask God to reveal any underlying fears and to equip you with the resources you need to overcome them. Pray for guidance in identifying the specific ways you can use your gifts to serve Him. Pray for protection against the negative thoughts and feelings that may try to discourage you. Establish a daily practice of prayer and meditation as a foundational element in your spiritual journey.

**Bible Study:** Immerse yourself in Scripture. Read stories of women in the Bible who used their gifts courageously, despite facing adversity. Let their examples inspire and encourage you. Meditate on verses that speak to courage, faith, and overcoming fear. Allow the wisdom of scripture to guide and strengthen your faith, and empower you to face any obstacles that may arise. Choose scriptures that address your specific fears and reflect on how they apply to your current situation.

**Mentorship:** Seek guidance from a wise, trusted mentor who can offer support, encouragement, and practical advice. Share your fears and concerns with them and ask for their prayers and insights. A mentor who has already walked this path can provide invaluable guidance, preventing you from repeating mistakes or unnecessarily struggling with challenges that have already been overcome. This mentorship will be a supportive environment where you can learn and grow.

**Community:** Surround yourself with a supportive community of believers who will lift you up, encourage you, and pray for you. Participate in church activities and fellowship groups, building relationships with people who will help you to grow in your faith and overcome your fears. A supportive community can offer encouragement, motivation, and accountability.

**Small Steps:** Start small. Don't try to do everything at once. Begin by using your gifts in a small, manageable way. As you gain confidence, gradually expand your service. Small successes build confidence and create momentum. Celebrate the achievements, no matter how minor they might seem.

**Self-Compassion:** Be kind to yourself. Remember that you are loved and accepted by God, regardless of your imperfections. Don't beat yourself up over mistakes or setbacks. Learn from your experiences and move forward with faith and hope. Recognize that setbacks are opportunities for growth, not failures.

**Focus on God's Glory:** Keep your focus on God and His glory. Remind yourself that you are serving Him, not yourself. Let His love and grace motivate you to use your gifts to bless others. This helps you to maintain the right perspective and avoid the pitfalls of pride or self-seeking. Remember that your efforts are about serving God and His kingdom, not personal recognition or achievement.

The journey of using your spiritual gifts may not be easy, but it is profoundly rewarding. As you overcome your fears and step into your God-given purpose, you will experience a deep sense of fulfillment and joy. You will discover a greater capacity for love, compassion, and service, and you will make a significant impact on the lives of others. Remember, God has not given you these gifts to hoard them but to use them to build His kingdom and bless the world around you. Your unique talents and abilities are essential elements of God's grand plan. Embrace your gifts with courage and allow God to lead you into a life of meaningful service. Trust in His power, His love, and His unwavering presence in your life. He will never forsake you, and the rewards of serving Him will far exceed any fear you may encounter along the way. The journey itself, marked by growth, faith, and obedience, is a significant blessing. Step into your calling, knowing the love and grace of God empowers you.

## Embrace the Call

Embracing your unique spiritual gifts is not merely about personal fulfillment; it's about actively participating in the grand tapestry of God's Kingdom. Each individual, woven into this intricate design, holds a vital and irreplaceable thread. To understand our role, we must first grasp the immense scope of God's plan – a plan that extends far beyond our individual lives and into the very fabric of eternity. We are not passive observers in this grand narrative; we are active participants, called to contribute our unique talents and abilities to the ongoing work of redemption and restoration.

This understanding shatters the limiting belief that our contributions are insignificant. Far from it, God's Kingdom thrives on diversity, on the varied gifts and talents that He has bestowed upon each of His children. Consider the human body: the eye cannot say to the hand, "I have no need of you," nor can the head say to the feet, "I have no need of you." Each part plays a vital role, and together they form a complete and functioning whole (1 Corinthians 12:21). This same principle applies to the body of

Christ – the church. We are each a unique part, essential to the overall functioning and health of the body.

The parable of the talents in Matthew 25:14-30 offers a powerful illustration of this principle. The master entrusts different amounts of talents (representing abilities and resources) to his servants, expecting them to use their gifts wisely. The servants who diligently invested their talents were commended and rewarded, while the servant who buried his talent was condemned for his inaction. This parable underscores the urgency and importance of utilizing our God-given gifts. It is not enough to simply possess these gifts; we are called to actively employ them for the advancement of God's Kingdom.

But how do we identify our specific role? The process of discerning our place within God's plan is a journey of self-discovery, prayer, and spiritual discernment. It involves seeking God's guidance through prayer, studying Scripture for insight, and seeking counsel from trusted mentors and spiritual leaders. It also requires honest self-reflection, acknowledging our strengths and weaknesses, and being open to the possibilities that God might place before us.

Recognizing our unique passions and talents is crucial in identifying our role. What activities bring us joy and a sense of fulfillment? What skills do we possess that could be used to serve others? These passions and talents often provide clues to our God-given purpose. Perhaps you have a knack for teaching, a gift for writing, a heart for counseling, or a talent for organizing. These skills, combined with a sincere desire to serve, can lead to opportunities to contribute meaningfully to God's Kingdom.

Another important aspect is considering our spiritual gifts. In 1 Corinthians 12, Paul outlines a range of spiritual gifts, including prophecy, teaching, serving, encouraging, giving, leading, and showing mercy. Reflecting on these gifts and honestly assessing our own strengths and inclinations can help us to discern our particular place within the body of Christ. Are you gifted in teaching God's word and making the Bible understandable to others? Do you have a gift for healing emotional or physical wounds in the lives of others? Perhaps you have the ability to lead people in prayer and worship. Are you naturally able to bring people together, building consensus and unity?

Once we have identified our spiritual gifts and passions, the next step is to actively seek opportunities to use them in service to God. This may involve volunteering at a local church, participating in a mission trip, or simply reaching out to those in need within our own communities. It might involve leading a small group, teaching a Sunday school class, or mentoring younger believers. The possibilities are endless, and the key is to be open to the opportunities that God presents.

Embracing our role in God's Kingdom often requires stepping outside of our comfort zones. We may face challenges, obstacles, and even setbacks along the way. There may be moments of doubt, fear, or uncertainty. But it is in these moments that our faith is tested and strengthened. We must remember that God does not call the equipped; He equips the called. He will provide the necessary strength, guidance, and resources to fulfill the tasks He has set before us.

Furthermore, it's crucial to understand that our role in God's Kingdom is not static. It can evolve and change over time as our gifts and circumstances change. What may be our primary focus at one stage in our lives may become secondary later, and vice versa. God often leads us on a path of continuous growth and development, challenging us to stretch our abilities and step into new areas of service. This journey of growth and discovery is part of the unfolding of God's plan in our lives.

The importance of humility and collaboration should also be emphasized. While recognizing and utilizing our own unique gifts is essential, we must also recognize the gifts and contributions of others. We are part of a team, working together to achieve a common goal. Collaboration, mutual support, and a spirit of humility are crucial for the effective functioning of God's Kingdom. Each individual's role is vital, and together, in unity and love, we can accomplish far more than we ever could alone.

Finally, remember that serving in God's Kingdom is not about personal gain or recognition. It's about glorifying God and impacting the lives of others. As we humbly offer our gifts and talents, we become instruments of God's grace, bringing hope, healing, and transformation to a world in desperate need. The rewards of serving are immeasurable, far exceeding any personal satisfaction or worldly accolades. The true reward lies in the knowledge that we have been used by God to further His Kingdom and make a difference in the lives of others. This is a life of profound purpose and eternal significance. Let us embrace our roles with joy, faith, and unwavering devotion to our Heavenly Father. The journey may be challenging, but the rewards are eternal.

## Discussion Questions

1. What unique talents or spiritual gifts do you believe you possess, and how have they manifested in your life?

2. In what ways have you experienced God's presence and empowerment in your daily activities or struggles?

3. How can you differentiate between your natural talents and your spiritual gifts?

4. Reflect on a time when you felt a strong sense of fulfillment or purpose. What were you doing at that moment, and what gifts do you think were at work?

5. How can journaling your thoughts and experiences help you identify your spiritual gifts?

6. What specific prayers or contemplative practices can you engage in to seek clarity on your unique gifts?

7. Have you read any specific scriptures about spiritual gifts? Which passages resonate with you and why?

8. How can feedback from mentors or spiritual advisors contribute to your understanding of your spiritual gifts?

9. What roles or responsibilities in your church or community have you tried, and what did you learn about your abilities through those experiences?

10. Why do you think it's important to use your spiritual gifts for the benefit of others rather than for personal gain?

11. How can you embrace opportunities for service as a means to discover your potential and gifts?

12. What fears or hesitations do you have about stepping into areas where you believe your gifts may be utilized, and how can you overcome them?

# CHAPTER 9
## OVERCOMING OBSTACLES AND CHALLENGES

The path to fulfilling God's purpose is rarely a smooth, straightforward journey. Along the way, we inevitably encounter obstacles, and among the most formidable are discouragement and doubt. These insidious enemies can chip away at our resolve, whispering insidious lies that undermine our faith and confidence in God's plan for our lives. They can leave us feeling overwhelmed, inadequate, and utterly alone in our struggle. But remember, these feelings are not unique to you. Many women, even those who have seemingly achieved great things in ministry or their personal lives, have wrestled with discouragement and doubt. The key is not to avoid these feelings but to learn how to navigate them effectively, drawing strength from our faith and the unwavering support of our community.

One common cause of discouragement stems from unmet expectations. We may set ambitious goals for ourselves, driven by a desire to please God and make a significant impact. However, when we fall short of those goals or when our efforts seem to yield little fruit, it's easy to become discouraged. We may start questioning our abilities, worthiness, and even God's plan for our lives. This is where a vital shift in perspective is needed. We must remember that God's assessment of our worth is not based on our achievements but on His immeasurable love for us. Our value is intrinsic; it's not dependent on our accomplishments. He sees our hearts, our intentions, and our unwavering commitment to Him, even when our outward progress feels slow or insignificant.

Furthermore, comparing ourselves to others is a surefire recipe for discouragement. Social media, in particular, can exacerbate this issue. We see carefully curated images of others' accomplishments, often overlooking the struggles and challenges they faced along the way. This creates a distorted reality, leading us to believe everyone else thrives while we struggle. This comparison breeds feelings of inadequacy and self-doubt. The antidote to this toxic comparison is a conscious and deliberate effort to focus on our own individual journey. We are not in competition with anyone; we are each on our own unique path, uniquely equipped by God for the specific tasks He has set before us.

Another significant source of discouragement stems from criticism and opposition. As women step into leadership roles or embrace their calling with passion and conviction, they inevitably encounter resistance. This opposition might come in the form of blatant criticism, subtle undermining, or even outright hostility. Some may dismiss your ideas or downplay your contributions. Others may question your motives or even attack your character. The sting of such negativity can be profound, leading to feelings of hurt, isolation, and discouragement. In these moments, it's crucial to remember that criticism doesn't necessarily reflect the truth. Often, the critic's words stem from their own insecurities or limitations. Seek out the counsel of trusted mentors and fellow believers to help you discern constructive criticism from harmful negativity.

Remember, you are not alone. God is your ultimate advocate, and He equips you to navigate these difficult waters.

Doubt, a close companion to discouragement, often manifests as questions about God's presence and guidance. When faced with seemingly insurmountable challenges, it's natural to question His plan for our lives. We may struggle to understand why certain circumstances are occurring or why prayers seem unanswered. These questions can be painful, yet they are a sign of our faith and not its absence. Genuine faith involves wrestling with doubt, not avoiding it. Engage in honest conversation with God, expressing your doubts and fears without reservation. His presence remains constant, even when we struggle to feel it.

Overcoming discouragement and doubt requires a multi-faceted approach. First, nurture your spiritual life. Spend time in prayer, meditating on scripture, and seeking guidance through worship. Engage in spiritual disciplines such as journaling, fasting, and solitude. These practices deepen our relationship with God, strengthening our faith and giving us the resolve to persevere in the face of adversity. Secondly, cultivate strong relationships with other believers. Find a supportive community of women who can offer encouragement, accountability, and prayer. Sharing your struggles with others can alleviate feelings of isolation and provide valuable perspective. Surrounding yourself with people who lift you up will strengthen your resilience during times of difficulty.

Remember the power of self-compassion. Be kind to yourself. Treat yourself with the same grace and understanding that you would offer a dear friend struggling with similar challenges. Acknowledge your feelings without judgment. It's okay to feel discouraged or doubtful; it's part of the human experience. Do not let these feelings define you or dictate your actions.

Lastly, practice gratitude. Even in difficult times, there is always something to be thankful for. Focusing on what you have rather than what you lack shifts your perspective and fosters a more positive outlook. Make a conscious effort to list things for which you are grateful each day. This practice will help you see the blessings amidst the challenges.

The journey of faith is not a sprint, but a marathon. There will be times of exhilaration and triumph, as well as times of discouragement and doubt. Embrace the entire spectrum of emotions, understanding that they are a part of God's process in shaping you. Remember that God's grace is sufficient, and His strength is made perfect in weakness (2 Corinthians 12:9).

Trust in His unwavering love, and He will carry you through the storms, strengthening your faith and leading you to the fulfillment of His perfect plan for your life. Embrace your struggles, for they are opportunities for growth and a deeper understanding of God's unwavering love. He doesn't promise an easy path, but He does promise His unwavering presence and strength to sustain you through every trial. Continue to seek Him, trust Him, and rely on Him. He will see you through. Your faith, your strength, and your perseverance will testify to the power of God's grace in your life. And through it all, His love endures.

Remember the words of Psalm 23:4: "Even though I walk through the darkest valley, I will fear no evil, for you are with me; your rod and your staff, they comfort me." Let these words be a source of comfort and strength as you navigate the challenges of life. Know that you are not alone; God walks with you every step of the way. Your resilience, your faith, and your perseverance will bear fruit in His time. Do not give up. Continue to trust in His plan, and embrace the journey with courage, grace, and unwavering faith.

**Thorns in the Roses**

The journey toward fulfilling God's purpose is rarely without its thorns. While discouragement and doubt can subtly erode our resolve, criticism, and opposition present a more direct and often painful challenge. Stepping into leadership, boldly proclaiming your faith, or simply living a life guided by Christian principles can invite scrutiny and even hostility. This opposition isn't a sign of failure; it's often a testament to the impact you're making. The very act of challenging the status quo, of living authentically in a world that often values conformity over conviction, can stir up resistance.

Understanding the source of this opposition is the first step towards navigating it effectively. Sometimes, criticism stems from genuine concern, even if it's poorly expressed. Perhaps your methods are questionable, or your approach needs refinement. Constructive criticism, while potentially painful, offers opportunities for growth and improvement. Learn to discern the difference between heartfelt concern and malicious attacks. A critical spirit aimed at tearing you down rather than building you up doesn't warrant the same response as genuine feedback. Prayerful discernment is crucial in determining the intent behind the criticism. Ask God for wisdom to understand the heart of the critic and the message within their words.

However, often criticism is rooted in the critic's own insecurities, prejudices, or misunderstandings. Fear, jealousy, or a lack of understanding can fuel opposition. People may feel threatened by your success, your confidence, or your unwavering faith. They may cling to misinformed views or be resistant to change, projecting their own anxieties onto you. In these cases, remember that their criticism reflects more about them than about you. Their negativity is a reflection of their internal struggles, not a judgment on your worth or capabilities.

Responding to criticism with grace and wisdom requires a Christ-like approach. Jesus himself faced immense opposition and criticism, yet he responded with love, compassion, and unwavering faith. He never retaliated with anger or bitterness. Instead, he demonstrated the transformative power of forgiveness and understanding. His example serves as a powerful guide for navigating difficult situations. Consider his words in Matthew 5:44: "But I tell you, love your enemies and pray for those who persecute you." This isn't a passive resignation to injustice; it's an active choice to respond with love, even in the face of adversity.

This doesn't mean you should passively accept every criticism or tolerate mistreatment. Setting healthy boundaries is essential. You have a right to protect your emotional and spiritual well-being. Learning to say no and politely decline requests that drain you or compromise your values is a crucial part of self-care and self-preservation. Don't feel obligated to justify your actions or beliefs to everyone. Your primary accountability lies with God, not with those who criticize you.

**Pray for your critics:** This doesn't mean you condone their actions; it means you are choosing to bless them, releasing any bitterness or resentment you might feel. Prayer can soften your heart and enable you to respond with empathy and understanding. Ask God to reveal their motivations and to show you how to respond with grace.

**Seek wise counsel:** Confide in trusted mentors, spiritual advisors, or fellow believers who can offer an objective perspective and prayerful support. They can help you discern constructive criticism from destructive attacks and guide you in formulating a thoughtful response. Avoid venting to everyone you know; instead, choose a few trusted confidantes who can offer encouragement and practical advice.

**Document unjust accusations:** If faced with persistent or malicious criticism, keep a record of the events. This documentation can be helpful if the situation escalates and requires further intervention. This is primarily for self-protection and is not about seeking revenge.

**Focus on your calling:** Remember why you embarked on this journey in the first place. Your purpose is rooted in God's plan for your life. Don't allow others' negativity to derail you from your calling. Maintain your focus on serving God and fulfilling His purposes.

**Practice self-compassion:** Be kind to yourself. Allow yourself to feel the hurt and disappointment without self-criticism. Remember that God's love is unconditional and that your worth is not determined by the opinions of others. Engage in self-care activities that nurture your physical, emotional, and spiritual well-being.

**Celebrate your victories:** Acknowledge your accomplishments, both big and small. Recognize God's hand in your successes and allow yourself to feel a sense of pride and gratitude for the work He's done through you. This celebration is not about boasting but about acknowledging God's faithfulness.

**Remember God's promises:** He is your ultimate advocate and source of strength. Lean on His promises for comfort and guidance, trusting that He will work all things together for good (Romans 8:28). Meditate on scriptures that speak to His faithfulness and unwavering love.

### Dealing with Opposition

Opposition can take many forms—from subtle undermining to blatant attacks on your character. You might encounter resistance from colleagues, church members, family, or even friends. The forms of opposition can be subtle. It might be a constant stream of passive-aggressive remarks or the deliberate exclusion from important decisions or events. It might be a whispering campaign to discredit you, or the intentional spreading of false information. It could even manifest as a complete lack of support or encouragement, leaving you feeling isolated and alone in your ministry or your efforts.

Dealing with these subtle forms of opposition requires wisdom, discernment, and often, quiet persistence. Don't be drawn into petty arguments or retaliatory actions. Instead, continue to conduct yourself with integrity, demonstrating your competence, your compassion, and your commitment to your calling. Your actions will speak louder than any whisper campaign. Remember, your faithfulness is a powerful testimony, even when it's not outwardly recognized.

In dealing with overt opposition, it's important to approach each situation with prayer and discernment. Sometimes, a direct conversation might be necessary but always approach it with a spirit of humility and willingness to listen. However, if the opposition becomes hostile, abusive, or threatening, it might be necessary to seek support from authorities or legal counsel. Your safety and well-being are paramount.

Ultimately, the key to overcoming criticism and opposition lies in your unwavering faith in God. Trust in His plan for your life, even when things are difficult. Remember that He equips you with the strength and resilience to face any challenge. Your faith, your strength, and your perseverance will testify to the power of God's grace in your life. And through it all, His love endures. His love will sustain you, guide you, and empower you to navigate the storms with grace and unwavering faith. Let His love be your strength, your shield, and your ultimate victory. Remember, He has called you, equipped you, and will see you through. Your journey is not in vain. His purpose will prevail.

Navigating the complexities of human relationships, especially within the context of faith and ministry, often presents significant challenges. While we strive to reflect Christ's love in all our interactions, we inevitably encounter individuals who test our patience, challenge our beliefs, or even actively work against our efforts. This is not a sign of personal failure; rather, it's a reality of living in a fallen world. However, we are not left to navigate these difficult relationships alone. God provides us with the wisdom, strength, and grace to overcome obstacles and maintain our spiritual well-being.

One of the most critical aspects of managing difficult relationships is establishing and maintaining healthy boundaries. This doesn't imply coldness or detachment; instead, it's about protecting our emotional, spiritual, and even physical well-being. It's about recognizing our limits and refusing to allow others to cross them. This might mean saying "no" to requests that drain our energy or compromise our values, even if it risks disappointing someone. It could involve limiting contact with individuals who consistently bring negativity into our lives. It might even necessitate removing ourselves entirely from toxic situations. This is not selfishness; it's self-preservation – a vital act of self-care that allows us to continue serving God effectively.

Effective communication is another crucial element in navigating challenging relationships. This doesn't necessarily mean confronting every conflict directly; sometimes, silence or carefully chosen words can be more powerful. However, when a direct conversation is necessary, we must approach it with a spirit of humility, empathy, and a willingness to listen. Before speaking, we should take time to pray for guidance, seeking God's wisdom to discern the best approach. When engaging in conversation, we should focus on expressing our own needs and feelings clearly and respectfully, without resorting to accusations or judgment. Active listening – truly hearing and understanding the other person's perspective – is essential. It might be that the conflict arises from a misunderstanding, and open communication can bridge that gap. Even if the conflict remains, a respectful exchange can at least create a healthier dynamic.

Forgiveness, a cornerstone of the Christian faith, is vital in navigating difficult relationships. Forgiving someone doesn't mean condoning their actions or minimizing the hurt they caused; it means releasing the bitterness and resentment that can poison our hearts and hinder our spiritual growth. Holding onto anger or unforgiveness only hurts us; it drains our energy and prevents us from moving forward. Forgiveness, however, is a process, not an event. It may take time and effort, perhaps even seeking guidance through prayer or counseling. The process may involve several steps, including acknowledging the hurt, releasing the desire for revenge, and choosing to extend compassion and grace. It's important to remember that forgiveness is ultimately an act of love, not a sign of weakness.

When dealing with persistent conflict or abuse, we must recognize that setting boundaries may not be enough. Seeking external support becomes necessary. This could involve confiding in a trusted friend, family member, mentor, or spiritual advisor who can provide emotional support, guidance, and prayer. If the situation involves abuse of any kind, we should seek professional help by contacting appropriate authorities, such as law enforcement or social services. Our safety and well-being are paramount, and we should not hesitate to seek help when needed.

In addition to the practical strategies outlined above, it's vital to cultivate a deep and abiding relationship with God. He is our ultimate source of strength, wisdom, and comfort. Spending time in prayer, studying scripture, and engaging in spiritual practices such as Bible meditation or journaling can provide the solace, guidance, and resilience we need to navigate difficult relationships. During challenging times, we should remind ourselves of God's unconditional love, His unwavering faithfulness, and His promises to be with us always. Meditating on scriptures like Psalm 23 ("The Lord is my shepherd, I lack nothing...") or Philippians 4:6-7 ("Do not be anxious about anything, but in every situation, by prayer and petition, with thanksgiving, present your requests to God. And the peace of God, which transcends all understanding, will guard your hearts and your minds in Christ Jesus.") can provide comfort and strength.

Furthermore, fostering a strong support system is crucial. Surrounding ourselves with positive and uplifting individuals who offer encouragement, understanding, and prayer is essential in overcoming challenges. This could involve attending a supportive church community, joining a small group, connecting with a mentor, or cultivating close relationships with fellow believers. These individuals can offer a listening ear, practical advice, and spiritual encouragement, helping us navigate difficult relationships and maintain our faith.

Remember that the journey of faith is not always easy. We will encounter obstacles and challenges, including difficult relationships. However, God has not left us alone to face these challenges; He has equipped us with the resources and support we need to overcome them. By establishing healthy boundaries, practicing effective communication, extending forgiveness, seeking external help when necessary, cultivating a deep relationship with God, and nurturing a strong support network, we can navigate difficult relationships with grace, resilience, and unwavering faith, emerging stronger and closer to God. Our struggles can refine our character, deepen our faith, and ultimately, bring us closer to fulfilling God's purpose for our lives. The path may be challenging, but the destination, guided by God's unwavering love and grace, is worth the journey. Trust in His timing and His plan; He will carry you through.

## Supportive Christian Community

The journey of faith, as we've explored, is rarely a solitary one. While our individual relationship with God is paramount, He also designed us for community, for the mutual support and encouragement that strengthens our resolve and deepens our faith. The challenges we face, particularly within the context of ministry and leadership, are often best navigated not alone, but within the embrace of a supportive Christian community. This isn't simply about social interaction; it's about a strategic alliance of faith, where shared burdens are lightened, shared joys amplified, and shared prayers strengthened.

Think of the early church, depicted in Acts 2:42: "They devoted themselves to the apostles' teaching and to fellowship, to the breaking of bread and to prayer." Their community wasn't merely a social gathering; it was a vital lifeline, a network of believers mutually supporting one another through persecution, hardship, and the daily challenges of living out their faith. This model of mutual support remains powerfully relevant today. A strong Christian community isn't just a nice-to-have; it's an essential component of spiritual growth and resilience.

One of the most significant benefits of belonging to a supportive community is the provision of emotional support. The challenges we face, whether in ministry, family life, or personal struggles, can often be overwhelming. Feeling alone, isolated, and misunderstood can lead to discouragement, depression, and even burnout. A strong community offers a safe haven, a place where we can share our vulnerabilities without fear of judgment, and where we can find empathy, understanding, and a listening ear. Knowing that others understand, even if they haven't experienced the exact same struggles, provides an immense sense of comfort and validation. This shared experience of vulnerability creates a powerful bond of trust and solidarity. Within this space, we can unpack our burdens, process our emotions, and receive encouragement to keep moving forward.

Beyond emotional support, a supportive Christian community provides practical assistance. When faced with unexpected difficulties – illness, financial hardship, or family emergencies – practical help can make all the difference. A community that values mutual support will rally together, offering tangible help in the form of meals, childcare, financial aid, or simply a helping hand. This practical assistance alleviates some of the stress and pressure, allowing us to focus on addressing the challenges themselves. This practical support isn't just a temporary fix; it's a demonstration of God's love in action, a tangible manifestation of the body of Christ working together.

Spiritual encouragement is another crucial aspect of a thriving Christian community. When we're struggling spiritually, wrestling with doubt, or feeling disconnected from God, the encouragement and prayers of fellow believers can be incredibly powerful. A community can provide accountability, gently reminding us of our commitments and encouraging us to stay focused on our spiritual goals. Fellowship with others strengthens our faith, enabling us to draw on the combined strength of believers to navigate spiritual difficulties. Through shared scripture study, prayer meetings, and uplifting conversations, we are encouraged to persevere in our faith, even when facing adversity.

Furthermore, a strong Christian community provides opportunities for spiritual growth and development. Through mentorship, teaching, and mutual learning, we can deepen our understanding of God's word and grow in our faith. Community service opportunities also foster spiritual maturity as we serve others and put our faith into action. By actively participating in the life of the church, we become more deeply rooted in our faith and more equipped to face the challenges that life throws our way. This active engagement fosters a sense of belonging and purpose, preventing feelings of isolation and strengthening our spiritual identity.

Finding and engaging with a supportive Christian community requires intentionality. It's not enough to attend a church service; it requires actively seeking out relationships, participating in small groups or ministries, and being willing to serve others. Begin by praying for God's guidance in finding a community that aligns with your values and spiritual goals. Attend services at various churches and investigate the different ministries and small groups they offer. Don't be afraid to talk to other members, asking about their experiences and finding out whether the church fosters a sense of belonging and mutual support. Prayerfully ask God to guide you where you should be; He will lead you to the place you should be. The important thing is to find a place where you feel welcomed, accepted, and supported.

Once you've found a community you feel drawn to actively participate. Don't be a passive observer; get involved in activities, volunteer your time, and engage in conversations. Building relationships takes time and effort; don't get discouraged if it doesn't happen overnight. Be open, approachable, and willing to share your experiences and support others. Actively listening to others' stories and offering encouragement can help foster genuine connections. Remember that building strong relationships takes time, and consistency is key. Attend events regularly, reach out to individuals, and actively contribute to the life of the community.

It's crucial to understand that not all communities are created equal. Some may be more welcoming and supportive than others. If you find yourself in a community that is toxic, unsupportive, or even abusive, don't hesitate to seek a new one. Your spiritual well-being is paramount; you deserve to be in a place where you feel loved, accepted, and encouraged. Remember that God's love is unconditional, and He will guide you toward a community where you can thrive spiritually.

The benefits of a supportive Christian community extend far beyond simply overcoming obstacles; it's about cultivating a deeper relationship with God and with fellow believers. It's about experiencing the true meaning of the body of Christ, working together in love and mutual support. It's about growing in faith, sharing burdens, celebrating victories, and walking together on the journey of life. It's about finding a place of belonging where you feel seen, heard, and loved for who you are in all your imperfections.

Furthermore, the presence of a strong community counters the isolation that can lead to spiritual stagnation. Feeling disconnected from others can erode our faith and leave us vulnerable to temptation and discouragement. But within a supportive community, we are reminded that we are not alone in our struggles. We are part of a larger body, connected to God and to one another through the shared bond of faith. This shared faith strengthens our individual faith, providing resilience, hope, and unwavering support in the face of adversity. The community becomes a powerful instrument of God's grace, shaping us into stronger, more compassionate, and more spiritually mature individuals.

Consider the example of Esther in the Old Testament. While called to a seemingly impossible task, Esther was surrounded by Mordecai and other trusted individuals who supported her in her courageous acts. Her community provided her with the strength and wisdom needed to undertake her divine mission. This model of support and encouragement is echoed throughout scripture, highlighting the importance of community in fulfilling God's purpose. We are not designed to navigate the complexities of life and ministry alone; we are meant to do so together, drawing strength from one another, sharing burdens, and celebrating triumphs.

Searching for and cultivating a strong Christian community isn't a one-time event; it's an ongoing process of seeking, connecting, and nurturing relationships. It requires intentionality, patience, and a willingness to be vulnerable. But the rewards are immeasurable, leading to a deeper faith, stronger resilience, and a richer, more meaningful life lived in the service of God. This is not simply about finding a church; it's about finding a family, a spiritual family that walks alongside you, offering support, encouragement, and unwavering love on the journey of faith. Embrace the power of community; it is a gift from God, designed to equip and empower you for the challenges ahead. Remember that God's love is not just found in individual devotion; it's also expressed and experienced within the loving embrace of His community.

## Develop Resilience

Developing resilience, that inner strength that allows us to bounce back from setbacks and persevere through challenges, is not merely a desirable trait; it's a spiritual necessity for every woman called to serve God. It's the bedrock upon which we build our lives of faith, enabling us to withstand the inevitable storms and emerge stronger on the other side. This resilience isn't a magical quality bestowed upon the few; it's a skill cultivated through intentional practices rooted in our faith.

Our faith in God forms the foundation of our resilience. When faced with adversity, our tendency might be to question God's plan and to feel abandoned or forgotten. But it is precisely in these moments that our faith is tested and refined. Remembering God's unwavering love and faithfulness, even amidst suffering, is paramount. Leaning into His promises, found throughout scripture, allows us to find comfort, strength, and hope amidst the storm. The Psalms, in particular, offer a wealth of examples of individuals crying out to God in distress, finding solace, and, eventually, experiencing His deliverance. These aren't just ancient accounts; they are timeless examples of how to navigate adversity through faith.

One crucial aspect of developing resilience is cultivating a mindset of gratitude. It's easy to focus on the negative, to dwell on our problems and challenges, but gratitude shifts our perspective. By consciously focusing on the blessings in our lives, even amidst difficulties, we begin to cultivate a more positive outlook. This doesn't mean ignoring our struggles; rather, it means acknowledging both the challenges and the blessings and finding balance in our perspective. Keeping a gratitude journal and regularly listing things we are thankful for can significantly impact our emotional well-being and enhance our ability to cope with stress. This practice helps re-wire our brains to focus on the positive, reducing the power of negativity and enhancing our overall resilience.

Developing a strong support system is also integral to building resilience. As we discussed earlier, a supportive Christian community provides a crucial network of love, encouragement, and practical assistance. Surrounding ourselves with individuals who understand our faith and journey allows us to share our burdens, receive prayer, and find encouragement when we feel overwhelmed. These individuals can offer a listening ear, offer practical help, and remind us of God's unwavering presence. This support network isn't a luxury; it's a vital component of our spiritual and emotional well-being, providing a buffer against the harsh realities of life's challenges. Don't underestimate the power of community; it is a gift from God, designed to equip and strengthen us.

Self-care, often overlooked in the busy lives of women in ministry, is another critical element of resilience. It's not selfish to prioritize our physical, emotional, and spiritual well-being; it's essential. This includes adequate sleep, healthy nutrition, regular exercise, and engaging in activities that bring us joy and peace. It also involves setting healthy boundaries, learning to say "no" when necessary, and protecting our time and energy. Self-care is not a luxury; it is necessary to sustain our spiritual journey and maintain our resilience in the face of adversity. It's about recognizing our limits and actively choosing to prioritize our well-being. This might involve scheduling regular time for prayer and meditation, pursuing hobbies, or simply spending time in nature. The key is to identify what truly replenishes us and make it a regular part of our routine.

Learning to forgive both ourselves and others is essential for cultivating resilience. Holding onto resentment, anger, or guilt can weigh heavily on our hearts and hinder our ability to move forward. Forgiveness doesn't mean condoning harmful behavior; it means releasing the bitterness and allowing God to heal our wounds. This is a process, not a single event, and it often requires seeking professional help or guidance from trusted mentors or spiritual leaders. Forgiving ourselves for past mistakes is equally important, recognizing that we are all imperfect and prone to error. God's grace extends to us, and we must extend that same grace to ourselves. The process of forgiveness frees us from the emotional burden of past hurts, enabling us to move forward with greater clarity and peace.

Developing a growth mindset, focusing on learning and improvement rather than dwelling on failures, is vital for building resilience. Challenges and setbacks are inevitable; how we respond to them defines our resilience. Viewing challenges as opportunities for growth, learning from mistakes, and adapting our strategies allows us to move forward with renewed determination. Instead of succumbing to self-doubt or despair, we embrace the learning process, viewing failures as valuable lessons. This approach shifts our focus from the outcome to the journey itself, fostering perseverance and enhancing our ability to overcome obstacles. Cultivating a growth mindset requires consistent self-reflection, a willingness to learn from our experiences, and a belief in our ability to improve.

Finally, maintaining a strong spiritual discipline is essential for resilience. This includes regular prayer, Bible study, and participation in worship. These practices connect us to God, grounding us in His love and providing us with the strength we need to face challenges. Prayer is not merely a request for help; it's a conversation with God, a means of pouring out our hearts and finding comfort and guidance. Bible study provides a foundation of truth, reminding us of God's promises and His unwavering faithfulness. Worship connects us to the larger body of Christ, reminding us that we are not alone in our struggles. Engaging consistently in these spiritual disciplines nourishes our faith, providing the resilience we need to overcome obstacles and persevere in our journey.

In closing, the path to developing resilience is not a sprint but a marathon. It requires intentional effort, consistent practice, and unwavering faith in God. By embracing these practices – fostering faith in God, cultivating gratitude, building a strong support system, prioritizing self-care, learning to forgive, developing a growth mindset, and maintaining a strong spiritual discipline – we equip ourselves to face the inevitable challenges of life with courage, grace, and unwavering perseverance. Remember that God is our strength, our refuge, and our source of unwavering love. He equips us with everything we need to overcome obstacles and emerge victoriously. Embrace the journey, trust in His plan, and know you are stronger than you think. The path ahead may be challenging, but with God's grace and your unwavering commitment, you will not only survive but thrive. He has called you to greatness and He will empower you to fulfill your purpose. Embrace your strength, your resilience, and the incredible potential God has placed within you.

## Discussion Question

1. What are some common obstacles women face when pursuing their purpose, as discussed in the text?

2. How can unmet expectations lead to feelings of discouragement and doubt?

3. In what ways can social media negatively impact our self-perception and contribute to discouragement?

4. What strategies can we use to avoid comparing ourselves to others on our personal journeys?

5. How can we discern between constructive criticism and harmful negativity from others?

6. Why is it important to embrace our doubts in relation to our faith?

7. What practices can help deepen our spiritual life and strengthen our faith during challenging times?

8. How can building a supportive community of believers alleviate feelings of isolation?

9. What role does self-compassion play in overcoming feelings of discouragement and doubt?

10. Can you identify something you are grateful for in your life right now, even amid struggles?

# CHAPTER 10

# LIVING A PURPOSE-DRIVEN LIFE

Having established the foundational principles of resilience, let's now turn our attention to a crucial aspect of living a purpose-driven life: setting intentional goals. This isn't about simply making a wish list; it's about strategically aligning our aspirations with God's purpose for our lives. Many women, particularly those involved in ministry, often feel overwhelmed by the sheer volume of tasks and responsibilities before them. They may find themselves juggling multiple roles—wife, mother, ministry leader, community volunteer—leaving little time for personal reflection and goal setting. However, setting intentional goals isn't a luxury; it's necessary to effectively utilize our time, talents, and energy. It provides a roadmap for navigating the complexities of life and fulfilling our divine calling.

The first step in setting intentional goals is prayerful reflection. This isn't a rushed, five-minute prayer before bed; it's a dedicated time to seek God's guidance and discern His will for our lives. This involves journaling, spending time in nature, engaging in quiet contemplation, or seeking guidance through prayer with trusted mentors or spiritual leaders. Through these practices, we open ourselves to the promptings of God, allowing Him to illuminate our path and reveal the specific goals He has for us. This is not about forcing our will upon God; it's about humbly seeking His direction and aligning our desires with His perfect plan.

Once we've spent time seeking God's guidance, we can begin to articulate our goals. It's important to be specific and measurable. Instead of a vague goal like "improve my ministry," we might set a goal like "Develop and deliver three new Bible study lessons on the book of Proverbs by the end of the year." This specific, measurable goal allows us to track our progress and celebrate our achievements. We can break down larger, more complex goals into smaller, more manageable steps. This approach helps prevent feeling overwhelmed and allows us to celebrate incremental progress along the way. Remember, the journey of faith is a marathon, not a sprint.

When setting goals, it's essential to consider our strengths and weaknesses. We should focus on areas where we excel, utilizing our gifts and talents to maximize our impact. However, we shouldn't shy away from areas where we need growth. These areas often represent opportunities for spiritual development and can lead to significant personal transformation. Setting goals in these areas requires a spirit of humility and a willingness to learn and grow. It's about embracing the process of personal development and recognizing that God uses challenges to refine and shape us into the women He created us to be.

Furthermore, it's critical to align our goals with our values. What are the principles that guide our lives? What is most important to us? Our goals should reflect these values, ensuring our actions are consistent with our beliefs. For instance, if we value service to others, our goals might include volunteering at a local homeless shelter or mentoring young women in our community. If we value spiritual growth, our goals must include upping prayer time, engaging in daily Bible study, or seeking spiritual direction. Aligning our goals with our values ensures we live a life of integrity and purpose.

Time management is crucial for achieving our goals. This often requires setting priorities and learning to say "no" to commitments that don't align with our goals. It's about being intentional with our time, protecting it from distractions and commitments that don't serve our purpose. This might involve delegating tasks, setting boundaries, or simply learning to say "no" to requests that drain our energy or compromise our goals. Remember, you are not responsible for everyone else's needs. It's a loving act to prioritize your spiritual well-being and ensure you effectively utilize your time and energy. This is not to say act selfishly, but to know when to say "no" and when someone really needs you.

Accountability is another vital element in achieving our goals. Sharing our goals with a trusted mentor, friend, or spiritual leader provides an external source of support and encouragement. They can offer advice, provide guidance, and hold us accountable for our progress. This doesn't mean we should feel pressured or judged; rather, it's about having a supportive network that encourages us to stay focused and persevere. The power of accountability, particularly within a supportive Christian community, can significantly increase the likelihood of achieving our goals.

Finally, we must remember that setbacks are inevitable. Life is not a linear progression; we will encounter challenges and obstacles along the way. When setbacks occur, it's essential to maintain a positive attitude and persevere. This requires faith, resilience, and a willingness to learn from our mistakes. Setbacks are opportunities for growth; they allow us to refine our strategies, adjust our approach, and emerge stronger on the other side. It is crucial to approach these moments with God's perspective, recalling his faithfulness and remembering that he uses even our mistakes for good.

Setting intentional goals is a spiritual discipline. It's a process of aligning our desires with God's will, utilizing our gifts and talents, and living a life of purpose and integrity. It requires prayerful reflection, clear articulation of goals, effective time management, a supportive accountability network, and a resilient spirit. It's a journey of growth and transformation, leading us to a deeper relationship with God and a greater understanding of our purpose in the world. Remember, God has a plan for your life; through prayer and intentionality, you can discover and fulfill that plan. His grace empowers us, enabling us to overcome obstacles and achieve our goals. Embrace the process, trust in His guidance, and celebrate the journey. The rewards of living a purpose-driven life are immeasurable, leading to a life of fulfillment, joy, and lasting impact.

Setting goals isn't a one-time event; it's an ongoing process as we journey through life. Life circumstances change, our priorities evolve, and our understanding of God's purpose deepens. Therefore, regular review and adjustments to our goals are essential. This might involve re-evaluating our priorities, refining our strategies, or even abandoning goals that no longer align with our purpose. Flexibility and adaptability are crucial for maintaining a healthy and fulfilling life in our faith.

Furthermore, celebrating our achievements along the way is equally important. When we reach a milestone, we should acknowledge our accomplishments and thank God for His guidance and support. This positive reinforcement encourages us to continue striving for our goals and reinforces the belief in our ability to achieve what God has called us to do. This celebration can take many forms; it might be a quiet moment of prayer, a special dinner with loved ones, or a thoughtful act of service to someone in need.

In conclusion, setting intentional goals, while demanding, is an act of faith, a deliberate choice to align our lives with God's purpose. It's a dynamic process requiring regular evaluation, adaptation, and celebration. It's a testament to our trust in God's plan for our lives, a journey of faith that empowers us to make a significant and lasting impact on the world. Remember, you are called to greatness, and with God's guidance and your dedicated efforts, you can achieve the remarkable things He has planned for you. Embrace the journey, trust in His plan, and allow Him to guide your steps as you strive to live a truly purpose-driven life. The path may be challenging, but the destination—a life lived in alignment with God's will—is worth the effort. The rewards are far greater than any earthly accomplishment; they are a life filled with purpose, peace, and the profound joy of serving the God who loves us unconditionally. This intentional journey, rooted in faith and guided by prayer, will lead you to a life of profound meaning and impact—a testament to the incredible potential God has placed within you.

**Prioritize Your Life**

Prioritizing our spiritual lives isn't merely about attending church services or engaging in occasional prayer; it's about cultivating a deep, abiding relationship with God that permeates every facet of our existence. It's about weaving faith into the fabric of our daily lives, transforming our routines and perspectives, and allowing God's love to shape our responses to the challenges and joys life presents. For women, especially those in ministry, this intentional prioritization becomes even more critical, as the demands of leadership, family, and community can often overshadow the vital need for personal spiritual nourishment.

One effective strategy is establishing dedicated time for prayer and Scripture meditation. This doesn't necessitate lengthy sessions; even fifteen minutes of focused communion with God can profoundly impact our hearts and minds. Find a quiet space, free from distractions, where you can connect with God without interruption. This might be early in the morning before the day's demands begin, during your lunch break, or before bedtime. Experiment with different times to discover what suits your schedule and energy levels best. Consistency is key; even short, regular periods of prayer are more impactful than sporadic, lengthy ones.

Beyond formal prayer, integrate mindfulness into your daily activities. This involves approaching tasks and interactions with a conscious awareness of God's presence. As you perform mundane tasks—washing dishes, driving to work, or folding laundry—take a moment to acknowledge God's hand in your life. This mindful approach transforms ordinary actions into spiritual disciplines, infusing our daily routines with a sense of reverence and gratitude. Such moments of mindful awareness foster a deeper connection with God, enriching even the most routine aspects of our lives.

Scripture reading is another essential spiritual practice. The Bible offers wisdom, guidance, and encouragement, providing solace and strength in times of trial. Instead of approaching Bible reading as a chore, view it as an opportunity to commune with God through His Word. Start with shorter passages and focus on reflecting upon the meaning and relevance of the text to your life. Engage with a study Bible or commentary to gain a deeper understanding of the context and application of scripture. Joining a Bible study group can provide additional support and fellowship, enriching your understanding and providing opportunities for interaction and spiritual growth with like-minded women. Through consistent study, scripture nourishes the soul, guiding us toward a deeper understanding of God's love and His plan for our lives.

Fasting is a powerful spiritual discipline that many women find transformative. It doesn't necessarily involve abstaining from food; it can also entail fasting from certain activities or pleasures, like social media or television, to focus on prayer and spiritual reflection. Fasting creates space for increased spiritual awareness and heightened sensitivity to the Spirit of God. It's a time to draw closer to God, focusing your thoughts and energy on seeking His guidance and direction. Remember to approach fasting with prayerful intention and listen for the guidance of the Spirit of God on how to practice this spiritual discipline in a way that honors God and nourishes your well-being.

Regular participation in corporate worship is vital for strengthening our spiritual lives. The collective praise, fellowship, and instruction received during church services nurture our faith and remind us that we are part of a broader community of believers. It's important to find a church community where you feel spiritually nurtured and supported and where you can connect with others who share your faith and values. The encouragement, fellowship, and shared faith experience strengthen your own faith journey.

Beyond formal practices, prioritize acts of service. Serving others demonstrates our love for God and our neighbor, deepening our spiritual connection and fulfilling our purpose. Engage in volunteer work, mentor others, or simply offer a listening ear to a friend in need. These acts of kindness foster spiritual growth and connect us with the wider community, demonstrating our faith through tangible acts of love and compassion. Remember that service is not just an external act but also an internal transformation; it fosters humility, empathy, and gratitude.

Alongside structured practices, nurture your personal relationship with God through journaling. Use your journal as a space to record your prayers, reflections on scripture, and personal insights. It becomes a record of your spiritual journey, allowing you to trace God's work in your life. Reviewing your journals can be a powerful way to reflect on spiritual growth and God's faithfulness over time.

It provides a private space for honest reflection, where vulnerability and openness to God's guidance can lead to greater intimacy.

Another effective practice involves cultivating gratitude. Take time each day to reflect on the blessings in your life, big and small. This practice shifts our perspective, focusing our attention on God's goodness and fostering a spirit of thankfulness. Expressing gratitude through prayer or journaling enhances our spiritual well-being, reinforcing our awareness of God's abundant provision in our lives.

Remember, incorporating these practices doesn't require a complete overhaul of your schedule. Start with one or two, gradually integrating others as you feel comfortable. The key is consistency and intentionality. View these practices not as burdens but as opportunities to deepen your relationship with God and experience the transformative power of His love. Through dedicated time with God, consistent acts of service, and a grateful heart, we prioritize our spiritual lives, enabling us to live purposefully and impactfully in the world. It's not about perfection but about persistent pursuit, a journey of faith marked by devotion, growth, and grace.

Furthermore, remember the importance of seeking support and accountability within your faith community. Share your spiritual goals with a trusted mentor or friend, someone who can offer encouragement, guidance, and prayer. They can provide a safe space to share your struggles and celebrate your victories, strengthening your faith journey through shared experience and mutual support. Being part of a community that shares your values and spiritual goals enhances your growth and provides crucial support during challenging times. This sense of belonging is an essential component of living a purpose-driven life, ensuring your spiritual well-being is supported and nourished.

Finally, remember that prioritizing your spiritual life is not a race but a marathon. There will be days when you feel more connected to God and days when you feel distant. Be kind to yourself during those times; don't beat yourself up for falling short. Instead, acknowledge your imperfections, repent, and continue seeking God with a humble and contrite heart. The journey of faith is one of continuous growth and refinement, marked by both triumphs and setbacks. It's in those moments of struggle that we often grow the most, drawing closer to God through reliance on His grace and mercy. Your commitment to prioritizing your spiritual life is a testament to your faith, a declaration of your trust in God's plan for your life, and a commitment to living a life of purpose and joy. Remember that His grace is sufficient for all your needs.

The rewards of prioritizing your spiritual life are immeasurable. Not only will you experience a deeper relationship with God, but you will also discover increased resilience, strength, and peace amidst life's storms. You'll find yourself better equipped to navigate challenges, make wise decisions, and impact the world around you in powerful and meaningful ways. Your increased spiritual capacity translates into greater effectiveness in all areas of your life, whether in your family, your community, or your ministry work. Embrace the journey, trust in His guidance, and allow Him to lead you into a life of profound meaning, purpose, and unwavering joy. This is not simply a religious exercise; it is the foundation for living a truly fulfilling life, reflecting God's love and grace in every aspect of your being.

### Finding Balance

The demands of a purpose-driven life, especially for women juggling ministry, family, and personal responsibilities, often feel overwhelming. Feeling stretched thin is a common experience, leading to burnout and a sense of inadequacy. However, living a life fueled by faith doesn't necessitate sacrificing our well-being.

Instead, it requires intentional strategies for managing our time and energy effectively, enabling us to serve God and others without depleting our own resources. This involves cultivating a mindful approach to daily life, prioritizing tasks, and establishing healthy boundaries.

One crucial aspect of effective time management is identifying our peak productivity periods. Are you a morning person or a night owl? Understanding your natural energy rhythms allows you to schedule demanding tasks for times when your focus and energy are highest. For instance, if you're most alert in the mornings, dedicate that time to prayer, Bible study, or other spiritually enriching activities. Conversely, if your energy levels peak in the afternoon, schedule those same activities for that time. This approach ensures you're not fighting your natural inclinations but working *with* them to maximize your effectiveness.

Prioritization is equally important. Learning to distinguish between urgent and important tasks is a vital skill. Often, we get caught up in the urgent – emails, phone calls, minor crises – neglecting the truly important tasks that contribute to our long-term goals. Employing methods like the Eisenhower Matrix (urgent/important) can be helpful in sorting through your to-do list and focusing your energy on what truly matters. Identify your key spiritual goals and professional objectives, and schedule dedicated time to work towards them, even if it's just for short periods. Remember, consistency is more valuable than sporadic bursts of activity.

Delegation is another powerful tool often underutilized. Are you shouldering responsibilities that could be shared? Identifying tasks that others can handle effectively frees up your time and energy for more impactful activities. This applies both in your professional and personal life. In ministry, this could involve delegating tasks to team members or volunteers. It might involve asking family members to share household chores or childcare responsibilities at home. Learning to trust others and relinquish control can be challenging, but it is essential for preventing burnout and ensuring long-term sustainability in your purpose-driven endeavors.

Setting boundaries is crucial for protecting your time and energy. This involves learning to say "no" to requests that don't align with your priorities or exceed your capacity. It's not selfish to prioritize your well-being; it's essential for maintaining a healthy balance and fulfilling your calling. Establish clear boundaries regarding your work hours, family time, and personal spiritual practices. Communicate these boundaries clearly and respectfully to others, protecting your time and energy for the tasks that truly matter. This might involve setting specific times for responding to emails or limiting your social media usage to designated periods. Remember that boundaries are not walls but protective measures that allow you to flourish.

Beyond time management techniques, conserving energy requires mindful attention to our physical and emotional well-being. Adequate sleep, regular exercise, and a healthy diet are fundamental for sustaining energy levels and preventing burnout. Physical activity doesn't necessarily mean rigorous workouts; a brisk walk, some yoga, or a simple stretching routine can significantly impact your energy levels and mental clarity. Nourishing your body with whole foods and plenty of water and limiting processed foods and excessive caffeine or sugar will help you maintain consistent energy throughout the day.

Prioritizing rest is as crucial as prioritizing work. Regular periods of rest – whether it's a short break during the day or a full weekend off – are vital for preventing burnout and maintaining mental clarity. Avoid scheduling yourself to the point of exhaustion. Plan for downtime and engaging in activities that bring you joy and rejuvenation. This could be reading a good book, spending time in nature, engaging in a hobby, or simply relaxing with loved ones.

Mindfulness and self-compassion are equally essential. Practice self-care by paying attention to your emotional and mental well-being. Engage in activities that nurture your soul. This could involve spending time in nature, listening to soothing music, or engaging in creative pursuits. Learn to recognize signs of stress or burnout – such as fatigue, irritability, or difficulty concentrating – and take proactive steps to address them before they escalate. It is crucial to remember that self-compassion is not self-indulgence but rather a necessary act of self-preservation, essential for maintaining long-term effectiveness and preventing burnout.

Cultivating gratitude is a powerful way to shift perspective and appreciate the blessings in your life. Taking time each day to reflect on what you're thankful for, both big and small, can profoundly impact your emotional state, fostering a sense of peace and contentment. This practice helps you focus on the positive aspects of your life rather than dwelling on the challenges. It promotes a sense of abundance and perspective, making coping with stress easier and maintaining a positive outlook.

Remember that time management and energy conservation are not one-size-fits-all solutions. What works for one person may not work for another. Experiment with different techniques and strategies, adapting them to your individual needs and preferences. The goal is to create a sustainable system that allows you to live a purposeful life without sacrificing your well-being. The journey towards effective time management and energy conservation is an ongoing process, requiring consistent effort and adaptation.

It is also important to seek support and accountability from others. Share your struggles and successes with trusted friends, family members, or mentors. They can offer encouragement, practical advice, and much-needed emotional support. A supportive community provides a crucial safety net, allowing you to persevere even during challenging times. Don't hesitate to ask for help when needed; seeking support is not a sign of weakness but a testament to your wisdom and self-awareness.

Finally, remember that the goal isn't to achieve perfect efficiency but to live a life that honors both God and yourself. Striving for perfection can be counterproductive, leading to feelings of frustration and self-criticism. Instead, embrace imperfection and celebrate your progress, no matter how small. Remember that God's grace is sufficient, and His love is unconditional. Trust in His guidance and allow Him to lead you on this journey of purpose, grace, and abundant living. Your journey is a testament to your faith and commitment to serving Him; therefore, take care of yourself in this process, and your effectiveness and contribution will be all the more impactful. Remember to rest, pray, and seek the support of others in your journey toward a fully lived, purpose-driven life.

**I can do all things through him who strengthens me. (Philippians 4:13)**

Cultivating a life driven by purpose isn't a sprint; it's a marathon. And like any marathon runner knows, proper training and self-care are essential to completing the race—and to do so with strength and grace. The previous sections highlighted the importance of time management and setting boundaries, crucial elements in maintaining energy and preventing burnout. But true, sustained well-being extends far beyond efficient scheduling. It necessitates a broad approach, nurturing our physical, mental, and spiritual health as interconnected aspects of our overall wellness.

Let's begin with the physical. Our bodies are temples of the Holy Ghost and treating them with respect is an act of worship. This isn't about achieving a specific body image or conforming to societal beauty standards; it's about honoring the gift God has given us and ensuring we have the strength and energy to fulfill His calling. This means prioritizing adequate sleep. Most adults require seven to nine hours of quality sleep each night. Consistent sleep deprivation leads to decreased cognitive function, increased irritability, and a weakened immune system, directly impacting our ability to serve effectively. Establish a regular sleep schedule, creating a calming bedtime routine to signal your body it's time to rest. This might include a warm bath, devotional reading, or quiet prayer. Avoid screens for at least an hour before bed, as the blue light emitted from electronic devices can interfere with melatonin production, a hormone essential for sleep regulation.

Furthermore, regular physical activity is not merely about aesthetics; it's a crucial component of maintaining both physical and mental health. Exercise releases endorphins, natural mood boosters that combat stress and anxiety. It improves cardiovascular health, strengthens the immune system, and boosts energy levels. Finding an enjoyable activity is key to making it a sustainable part of your routine. This could be anything from brisk walking or jogging to swimming, dancing, or yoga. The goal is to find movement that brings you joy and helps you connect with your body. Even short bursts of activity throughout the day—taking the stairs instead of the elevator or walking during your lunch break—can contribute significantly to your overall health.

Nutrition plays an equally vital role. Nourishing our bodies with wholesome foods provides the fuel we need to thrive. A balanced diet rich in fruits, vegetables, whole grains, and lean protein sustains energy levels, sharpens mental focus, and strengthens the immune system. Limiting processed foods, sugary drinks, and excessive caffeine is essential for preventing energy crashes and mood swings. Consider incorporating mindful eating practices into your routine, paying attention to your food's taste, texture, and aroma. This can transform mealtimes from a hurried necessity into opportunities for gratitude and self-nurturing.

Beyond the physical, our mental and emotional well-being deserves equal attention. Stress, anxiety, and depression are common challenges in today's fast-paced world, particularly for women juggling multiple roles. Cultivating practices that promote mental and emotional resilience is therefore crucial. Regular prayer and meditation are powerful tools for calming the mind and connecting with God's peace. Prayer is not merely a request for help; it's a conversation with our Heavenly Father, a source of comfort, guidance, and strength. Through silent reflection, Scripture Meditation helps quiet the mind's chatter, allowing us to focus on the present moment and connect with our inner selves.

Journaling can be another valuable tool for processing emotions and gaining clarity. Writing down your thoughts and feelings can provide a sense of release and help you identify patterns of thinking and behavior. It's a private space where you can explore your emotions without judgment, allowing you to better understand yourself and your responses to life's challenges. Spending time in nature, engaging in hobbies, or pursuing creative pursuits are other ways to nurture your mental and emotional well-being. These activities offer opportunities for relaxation, self-expression, and connection with something larger than ourselves.

Spiritual health is the cornerstone of a purpose-driven life. It's about cultivating a deep and abiding relationship with God, grounding yourself in His love and grace. This involves consistent prayer and Bible study, practices that nourish our souls and guide our actions. It also involves actively seeking opportunities for spiritual growth, whether through attending church services, participating in small groups, or engaging in spiritual mentorship. Regularly engaging with scripture provides guidance and wisdom for navigating life's challenges, reminding us of God's unwavering love and faithfulness. Connecting with a community of faith that supports and encourages your spiritual journey is important.

Remember that spiritual growth isn't a solo endeavor. Surround yourself with people who uplift and inspire you, who share your faith and commitment to living a purpose-driven life. Participating in a church or small group allows fellowship, support, and accountability. It provides a space to share your struggles and celebrate your victories with others who understand your journey. Finding a mentor, someone who has walked a similar path can provide invaluable guidance and support. This person can offer wisdom, encouragement, and prayer, providing a lifeline during challenging times.

Cultivating healthy habits requires intentionality and consistency. It's not about achieving perfection but about making small, sustainable changes that contribute to your overall well-being. Start by identifying one area you'd like to improve, focusing on making small, incremental changes. Don't try to overhaul your entire life overnight; instead, focus on creating sustainable routines that you can maintain over time. Be patient with yourself; setbacks are inevitable. When you experience setbacks, don't get discouraged. Instead, view them as opportunities for learning and growth. Acknowledge your efforts, celebrate your progress, and remember that God's grace is sufficient for every challenge you face. Embrace the journey, trusting in God's guidance every step of the way.

This comprehensive approach—integrating physical, mental, spiritual, and emotional well-being—is not merely self-care; it is an act of spiritual discipline. It is recognizing that our bodies, minds, and spirits are intricately interwoven, and neglecting one impacts the others. By prioritizing our overall health, we are better equipped to live purposeful lives, radiating God's love and grace to those around us. We become more effective in our ministries, stronger in our relationships, and more resilient in the face of adversity.

Remember, the journey to a purpose-driven life is a process of continuous growth and refinement, a testament to our faith and commitment to serving God with our whole selves. Take care of yourselves, sisters, for you are warriors of God, and your well-being is essential to the work He has called you to do. Let's continue to rise with grace.

**Say "Yes" intentionally to those things that nourish your soul.**

The journey towards a purpose-driven life, as we've explored, is a marathon, not a sprint. We've established the foundational importance of time management and setting boundaries, but true, lasting fulfillment necessitates a deeper dive into the delicate dance of balance and the crucial art of preventing burnout. This isn't just about efficiency; it's about overall well-being, recognizing the interconnectedness of our physical, emotional, mental, and spiritual selves. Burnout, that insidious enemy of purpose, often creeps in subtly, manifesting as exhaustion, cynicism, and a sense of reduced personal accomplishment. It's a spiritual and emotional desert, leaving us feeling depleted and unable to serve God or others effectively. Avoiding this desolate landscape requires proactive measures and a conscious effort to establish healthy boundaries and prioritize self-care, not as a luxury, but as a sacred duty.

Setting boundaries is often misunderstood as selfish. It's frequently presented as a concept that clashes with the selfless nature of Christian service. However, setting healthy boundaries is an act of self-preservation, enabling us to serve more effectively and with greater compassion. It's about recognizing our limitations and honoring our need for rest and rejuvenation. Think of it as a gardener tending to their precious plants – one cannot relentlessly prune and harvest without allowing for periods of rest and replenishment. Similarly, we cannot pour endlessly from an empty well. Setting boundaries isn't about saying "no" to everything; it's about discerning what truly aligns with our purpose and what drains our energy and spirit. It's about saying "yes" intentionally, to those things which nourish our souls and allow us to flourish in our calling.

Consider your commitments – both professional and personal. Are you over-committed? Do you regularly find yourself feeling overwhelmed and stressed? If so, it's time to take stock and make some difficult choices. This might involve delegating tasks, saying "no" to additional responsibilities, or even reevaluating your current commitments. This might mean saying no to a committee position at church, turning down an extra volunteer shift, or politely declining a social invitation that will leave you feeling drained. This is not about being unkind; it's about being kind to yourself. It's about recognizing that saying "no" to one thing allows you to say "yes" to something far more important – your own well-being and your ability to effectively serve God.

Learning to say "no" gracefully requires practice. It's not about abruptly rejecting requests; instead, it's about expressing your limitations with kindness and honesty. For instance, instead of a simple "no," consider responses like: "Thank you for thinking of me. I'm currently overwhelmed with commitments and unable to take on any more at this time." or "I appreciate the invitation, but I need to prioritize self-care this week." These responses convey respect while clearly stating your limitations. Remember, your time and energy are precious resources, and you have the right to protect them. This isn't about self-centeredness but about responsible stewardship of the gifts God has given you.

Beyond setting boundaries, prioritizing self-care is equally crucial. This isn't about indulging in frivolous activities; it's about actively nurturing our physical, mental, and spiritual well-being. It's about consciously creating space for activities that nourish our souls and replenish our energy. This might involve spending time in nature, engaging in hobbies, reading inspirational books, or simply taking quiet moments for prayer and reflection. It might be taking a long bath, listening to uplifting music, or engaging in a creative pursuit – painting, knitting, writing – whatever brings you joy and allows you to disconnect from the demands of daily life. These seemingly small acts are powerful tools for combating burnout and preventing it from taking hold. They are acts of spiritual discipline.

Consider the integration of mindfulness practices into your daily routine. Mindfulness involves paying attention to the present moment without judgment. It's about being fully present in whatever you're doing, whether it's eating a meal, praying, or spending time with loved ones. This can help reduce stress and anxiety, improving your overall well-being. Simple mindfulness exercises, such as deep breathing or focusing on your senses, can be incredibly effective in calming the mind and reducing stress. Even short bursts of mindfulness throughout the day can have a significant impact. It's about cultivating an awareness of your inner self, connecting with your spirit, and finding moments of peace amidst the chaos of life.

Sleep deprivation is a significant contributor to burnout. Adequate sleep is essential for physical and mental restoration. Aim for seven to nine hours of quality sleep each night. Establish a regular sleep schedule, creating a relaxing bedtime routine to signal your body it's time to rest. Avoid screen time before bed, and create a sanctuary for sleep—a calming, dark, quiet space. This isn't a luxury; it's a necessity for effective ministry and service. Similarly, regular exercise is not merely about physical fitness; it's about mental and emotional health as well. Exercise releases endorphins, natural mood elevators that combat stress and anxiety. Find an activity you genuinely enjoy—walking, swimming, yoga, dancing—and make it a consistent part of your routine. Regular physical activity boosts energy levels and helps maintain a healthy weight, contributing to overall well-being.

Nourishing our bodies through healthy eating is just as important. A balanced diet rich in fruits, vegetables, whole grains, and lean protein fuels our bodies and minds. Limit processed foods, sugary drinks, and excessive caffeine. Mindful eating – paying attention to your food's taste, texture, and aroma – transforms mealtimes into opportunities for gratitude and self-care. Hydration is also crucial; ensure you are drinking plenty of water throughout the day. These seemingly simple adjustments significantly impact our energy levels and overall well-being. It's about making conscious choices to fuel our bodies with the nourishment they need to thrive.

Remember, finding balance and avoiding burnout isn't a one-time achievement; it's an ongoing process. It requires consistent effort and a commitment to prioritizing our well-being. It's about regularly assessing our commitments, setting healthy boundaries, and engaging in self-care practices that nourish our souls. It's about recognizing that our service to God is best served when we're healthy, rested, and spiritually grounded. It's an act of faith, believing in the importance of self-care as a critical component of living a truly purpose-driven life. It's about understanding that our well-being isn't selfish; it's an essential part of our spiritual journey, allowing us to serve with joy, energy, and grace for years to come. So, sisters, prioritize your well-being. It's not self-indulgence; it's spiritual survival. It's the pathway to fulfilling God's calling with unwavering strength and unshakeable grace.

## Discussion Questions

1. What are some specific ways you can seek God's guidance in setting your personal goals?

2. How do you differentiate between a vague goal and a specific, measurable goal in your life?

3. In what areas do you feel your strengths lie, and how can you leverage them in your goal-setting process?

4. Can you identify areas in your life where you need growth? How might these challenges contribute to your spiritual development?

5. What values are most important to you, and how do they influence the goals you set for yourself?

6. How do you practice effective time management to ensure you have space for your goals?

7. What strategies do you use to say "no" to commitments that do not align with your personal goals

8. Who in your life could serve as an accountability partner, and how can they support you in achieving your goals?

9. How do you plan to handle setbacks or challenges that may arise while pursuing your goals?

10. In reflecting on past experiences, what lessons have you learned from setbacks, and how can you apply those lessons moving forward?

# CHAPTER 11

# YOUR LEGACY OF FAITH

Leaving a positive impact isn't about grand gestures or monumental achievements; it's about the ripple effect of our daily choices, the quiet acts of kindness, and the consistent witness of our faith. It's about the legacy we leave behind – not just in terms of material possessions, but in the lives we touch and the hearts we inspire. As women of faith, we have a unique opportunity to shape the future and to leave a legacy that echoes through generations, influencing the lives of our children, grandchildren, and even those we may never meet. This legacy is not something passively inherited; it is actively cultivated, a testament to the life we choose to live.

Consider the women who have inspired you—grandmothers, mothers, mentors, or even historical figures. What is it about their lives that resonates with you? What qualities did they possess that you admire? These women, often unsung heroines, shaped the lives of others through their actions, their unwavering faith, and their unwavering commitment to their values. They left behind a legacy of strength, resilience, and faith that continues to impact those who followed. Their lives serve as a powerful reminder that our individual actions have a profound and lasting influence.

The foundation of a positive legacy rests on the principles of faith and integrity. Living a life rooted in our faith, guided by God's word and consistently striving to live out His teachings, is paramount. This is not a performance; it's an authentic expression of our relationship with God. Integrity—acting with honesty, compassion, and ethical behavior in all our interactions—is equally important. It is this integrity that builds trust and fosters genuine connections with others. It's in the steadfastness of our character and our unwavering commitment to our values that we lay the groundwork for a legacy of strength and moral uprightness.

Think about your daily interactions. Do you approach them with a spirit of generosity and love? A simple act of kindness, a listening ear, an offering of support—these are the small acts that often hold the greatest impact. We are called to be the hands and feet of Christ, reflecting His love in all that we do. These acts of service, woven into the fabric of our daily lives, build a legacy of compassion and grace that transcends time. It's in these quiet moments of service that we truly embody the essence of our faith, leaving a lasting impression on those whose lives we touch.

Mentorship plays a crucial role in shaping a legacy of faith. Taking the time to guide and support younger generations, to share our wisdom and experience, is an investment in the future. By nurturing the spiritual growth of others, we are not only fulfilling our own calling but also ensuring that the flame of our faith burns brightly in those who follow. Consider the women who mentored you. What impact did their guidance have on your life? How can you, in turn, provide that same support and encouragement to others? Mentorship is a powerful tool for leaving a legacy that extends far beyond our own lifetime.

Furthermore, actively participating in our communities is essential to shaping a meaningful legacy. This participation might involve volunteering at a local charity, supporting a cause close to our hearts, or simply being present and engaged in the lives of those around us. In our commitment to our communities, we leave behind a legacy of service, impacting the lives of those who live within our spheres of influence. These seemingly small contributions collectively build a stronger, more compassionate community. They embody the essence of Christ-like living, a testament to our faith manifested through selfless acts of service.

Building strong relationships is another vital component of leaving a positive legacy. Nurturing our relationships with family, friends, and colleagues requires intentional effort, time, and genuine care. These relationships provide support, encouragement, and a sense of belonging. They are the sources of strength, resilience, and joy. The strength of our relationships forms the bedrock of our legacies, shaping the memories and experiences that will be cherished long after we're gone. It's in the depth and richness of these bonds that we leave a legacy of love, connection, and belonging.

Beyond our interpersonal relationships, the written word can potentially leave a lasting legacy. Keeping journals, writing letters, or even creating a family history can preserve our thoughts, experiences, and values for future generations. These written accounts provide a window into our lives, offering insights into our faith, our struggles, and our triumphs. They serve as a lasting reminder of our impact on the world and serve to inspire future generations. Through writing, we create a tangible legacy that transcends the ephemeral nature of life itself.

Ultimately, leaving a positive legacy of faith is not a destination; it's a journey. It's a continuous process of striving to live a life that reflects God's love, compassion, and grace. It's in the small, everyday choices, our interactions with others, and our commitment to our faith that we shape the world around us, leaving a mark that extends far beyond our own lifespan. It's about living intentionally, with purpose and grace, leaving behind a tapestry of memories, experiences, and acts of kindness that will inspire and uplift those who follow. Let us embrace this opportunity, this sacred calling, to leave a legacy that glorifies God and inspires generations to come. This is not merely about our own fulfillment but about carrying the torch of faith, passing it on to future generations so they may continue to shine brightly. It's a legacy built not on fleeting achievements but on consistent devotion to Christ's teachings and the impact we have on the lives we touch.

**Faith Legacy isn't defined by worldly succuss**

The legacy we leave isn't defined by worldly success but by the depth of our faith and the breadth of our impact on others. Let us strive to be women of faith, compassion, and integrity, creating a ripple effect of goodness that extends through generations, leaving behind a lasting legacy that inspires and uplifts for years to come. This is our calling, our responsibility, and our privilege as daughters of God. Let us answer this call with unwavering dedication and a spirit of selfless service, creating a legacy that glorifies God and blesses the world around us. Our lives are not ours alone; they are a gift, a testament to God's grace, and a precious opportunity to leave a legacy of faith that will endure for generations to come.

Therefore, sisters, let us rise to the occasion, embracing the challenge of creating a legacy that extends beyond our own lifetime. Let us live lives of purpose, radiating God's love in all that we do, and leave behind a legacy that inspires and blesses for generations to come. It's not about accolades or recognition but the quiet impact we have on the lives we touch. It's a testament to our faith, a beacon of hope, and an enduring legacy of grace. Let us strive to make our lives a testament to God's unwavering love and the transformative power of faith. Let us live, not for ourselves alone, but for the generations to come, carrying the torch of faith and illuminating the path for those who follow. Our legacy is not merely a collection of achievements but a tapestry woven with threads of love, faith, and service – a masterpiece of God's grace, continuing to inspire and bless for generations to come.

Mentoring and discipling other women is not merely an act of kindness; it is a sacred responsibility, a vital component in weaving the rich tapestry of our spiritual legacy. It is an act of faith, a testament to the transformative power of God's grace, and a vital link in the chain of generations, ensuring that the flame of faith burns brightly for years to come. Consider the women who have shaped your life – grandmothers, mothers, teachers, mentors – who instilled in you a love for God and His word, guided you through life's storms, and celebrated your triumphs. Their influence, their unwavering faith, and their selfless devotion have left an indelible mark on your journey, shaping the person you are today. Now, it is our turn to extend that same grace and guidance to others.

The act of mentoring and discipling goes beyond simply imparting knowledge; it involves nurturing spiritual growth, fostering a deep and abiding relationship with God, and empowering others to discover and embrace their God-given potential. It's about cultivating a safe space where vulnerability is embraced, questions are encouraged, and faith is nurtured in its most authentic form. It's a journey of mutual growth, a reciprocal relationship where both mentor and mentee are enriched by the exchange of wisdom, experience, and prayer.

But where do we begin? How do we effectively mentor and disciple other women, ensuring that our efforts bear fruit, leaving a lasting legacy of faith and empowerment? Firstly, it requires a deep understanding of the word of God, and then the individual we're mentoring. Each woman walks a unique path, grappling with distinct challenges and possessing specific strengths and gifts. A one-size-fits-all approach will not suffice. Instead, we must invest time in getting to know them and understanding their spiritual journey, their aspirations, and their obstacles. Listening is paramount, creating a space where they feel comfortable sharing their vulnerabilities, hopes, and fears without judgment.

Active listening goes beyond simply hearing words; it involves truly understanding the heart behind the words. It involves observing body language, picking up on subtle cues, and creating a non-judgmental environment where they feel safe to be completely themselves. It's about engaging in empathetic listening, reflecting back their feelings and concerns to show that you truly understand their perspective. This establishes a foundation of trust and mutual respect, which is vital for any meaningful mentorship relationship.

Once you've established a strong connection based on trust, you can begin to guide and nurture their spiritual growth. This may involve studying scripture together, engaging in meaningful conversations about faith, or exploring different spiritual practices. Remember, discipleship is not a power dynamic but a partnership in faith. It is about walking alongside them, offering guidance and support rather than dictating their spiritual path. Consider using biblical examples to illustrate spiritual principles, allowing them to apply those principles to their lives. Sharing personal struggles and victories can also foster a deeper connection and demonstrate the ongoing nature of faith.

Practical application is crucial. Mentoring shouldn't remain confined to theoretical discussions; While biblical standards are important, it's vital to recognize that there are often deeper issues at play when someone feels stuck or trapped by oppression. To truly advance in their spiritual journey, individuals must address the underlying causes that are holding them back. Only by confronting these root issues can they find the freedom and growth they seek.

Understanding the power of active listening is vital in these situations. By asking thoughtful questions, you can uncover deeper insights into what might be blocking the other person, even if they aren't fully aware of it themselves. Building trust is fundamental when mentoring, so ensure your intentions are sincere. This isn't about gathering information for gossip; it's about genuinely wanting to help someone find their way out of their struggles. You could say, "I'm curious about your family life—can you share a bit about it?" or "Have you experienced any difficult times in your past that might still be affecting you today?" Your compassionate approach can truly make a difference.

This is an area where I was deeply let down by those around me, when they noticed my inability to let go of certain burdens. Despite their awareness, no one took the time to sit with me and explore what was holding me back. Then, I attended a weekend author's convention, which unexpectedly morphed into a transformative revival experience. It was at this gathering that a remarkable woman from California stepped into my life. With her warm presence and insightful guidance, she helped me unveil the underlying issues that had been holding me back for years. Her perspective was eye-opening and sparked a profound transformation within me. I went from feeling trapped by my past to embracing a renewed sense of purpose and freedom—an unforgettable journey that truly reshaped my life!

Engaging in heartfelt prayer and immersing yourself in the teachings of the word of God are crucial steps on your journey of personal and collective healing. Consider this: how can you effectively guide and support others if you lack clarity about your own mission or the signs you should be seeking? It's important to release any competitive thoughts that may linger in your mind, as they can become barriers to your growth and the growth of those around you.

We are each called to be compassionate shepherds, nurturing and enlightening one another as we navigate the complexities of healing. By sharing our knowledge, wisdom, and experiences, we can embark on a transformative journey together—one that inspires and uplifts, allowing us to extend our hands to those in need. Together, we have the power to create a ripple effect of healing that reaches far beyond ourselves, impacting our communities and the world.

Finally, remember that you, as a mentor, are not perfect. Be open about your own struggles and failures, demonstrating authenticity and humility. This allows your mentee to see faith not as a flawless performance, but as a continuous journey of growth and grace, marked by both triumphs and setbacks. Sharing your own vulnerabilities creates a safe space for your mentee to do the same, fostering a deeper connection and enhancing the mentorship experience. It allows them to see that faith is not about perfection but about striving toward God's love and grace.

Mentoring and discipling other women is a high calling, a privilege that echoes through generations. It's an investment in the future, a legacy of faith passed on to those who will carry the torch forward. It's about shaping lives, fostering spiritual growth, and leaving a lasting impact on the Kingdom of God. By embracing this opportunity, we not only empower others but we also enrich our own lives, experiencing the profound joy and fulfillment that comes from pouring our hearts and souls into the lives of other women. Let us rise to this challenge, embracing the responsibility and leaving behind a legacy of faith that will inspire and transform lives for generations to come. Let our lives be a testament to God's grace, a beacon of hope, and an enduring legacy of faith for those who follow in our footsteps.

## Be an Inspiration

Inspiring others to follow Christ isn't about grand pronouncements or dramatic gestures; it's about the quiet, consistent living out of our faith in everyday life. It's in the small acts of kindness, the unwavering commitment to prayer, the steadfastness in the face of adversity, and the genuine love we show to those around us that truly inspire others to draw closer to God. Think of the ripple effect: one act of kindness can inspire another, and another, creating a wave of positive influence that stretches far beyond our immediate circle.

Our lives are living testaments to God's grace, whether we realize it or not. Every challenge overcome, every moment of forgiveness given, every act of selfless service – these are all opportunities to showcase the transformative power of God's love. When we allow God to work through us, our lives become beacons of hope, guiding others toward a deeper understanding of His grace and mercy.

Consider the lives of women in scripture: Esther, who risked her life to save her people; Ruth, who demonstrated unwavering loyalty and faithfulness; Deborah, a courageous leader who led her people to victory; and Hannah, whose persistent prayer was answered in a miraculous way. These women, despite facing immense challenges, remained steadfast in their faith, leaving a powerful legacy that continues to inspire us today. They didn't preach sermons; they lived lives that spoke volumes. Their actions were their sermons.

How, then, can we, in our own lives, become living examples of faith, inspiring those around us? It begins with a deep and abiding relationship with God. This isn't merely a Sunday morning affair; it's a daily commitment to prayer, to Bible study, to seeking God's guidance in every aspect of our lives. The more intimately we know

God, the more naturally our faith will shine through in our actions and attitudes. It is in these quiet moments of communion that we find the strength and inspiration to navigate the complexities of life, and to share that strength with others.

This intimate connection with God allows us to cultivate an attitude of gratitude, recognizing God's hand in every aspect of our lives, even the difficult ones. This doesn't mean ignoring pain or hardship but rather acknowledging that even in the midst of struggle, God is working for our good, shaping us into women of resilience, faith, and compassion. When we express gratitude, even amidst trials, we demonstrate a faith that inspires others to find hope in their own circumstances.

Furthermore, intentionally living a life of service is crucial. Serving others, whether through volunteering at a local charity, mentoring a younger woman, or simply offering a listening ear to a friend in need, demonstrates the love of Christ in tangible ways. These acts of service are not merely acts of charity; they are expressions of our faith, tangible representations of God's love pouring out through us. When we serve others selflessly, we become living examples of Christ's teachings, inspiring others to follow in His footsteps.

Authenticity is paramount. We cannot inspire others by pretending to be someone we are not. Our imperfections, our struggles, our moments of doubt – these are all part of our journey of faith. Sharing our vulnerabilities with others, not as a means of seeking pity but as a testament to God's unwavering love and grace, creates a space for others to share their own struggles without shame or fear of judgment. This vulnerability fosters trust and connection, creating a safe haven for open and honest conversations about faith and life's challenges.

Forgiveness is a powerful tool in inspiring others. Forgiving others, even when it is difficult, releases us from the bitterness and resentment that can weigh us down. It is an act of faith, a demonstration of God's grace extending through us to others. By choosing to forgive, we model Christ's example of unconditional love, inspiring others to let go of their own hurts and embrace a life of peace and reconciliation.

In addition to these personal practices, we can actively seek out opportunities to share our faith. This might involve engaging in conversations about faith with friends, family, and colleagues, joining a small group or Bible study, or participating in outreach programs within our communities. The key is to do so with grace, respect, and a genuine desire to share the transformative power of Christ's love. It's not about **proselytizing**; it's about sharing our experiences, our testimonies, and our joy in knowing Christ in a way that naturally draws others to Him.

Consider your workplace. How can you demonstrate your faith in your daily interactions with colleagues? It might be as simple as showing kindness, offering a helping hand, or maintaining a positive attitude even during stressful times. By demonstrating Christ-like qualities in your professional life, you can subtly yet powerfully impact the lives of those around you. Your integrity, your work ethic, your compassion – all these are expressions of your faith.

Within your family, strive to create a home where faith is nurtured and celebrated. Engage in family prayer, attend church services together, and instill Christian values in your children. Your family is your first and most significant audience, and your example will profoundly shape their spiritual development and their understanding of faith. Create a space of love, acceptance, and understanding, where faith is lived and shared openly and honestly.

The power of a living example cannot be overstated. Our lives are not merely our own; they are a reflection of God's grace, a testament to His power, and an inspiration to those who witness them. By living out our faith consistently and by demonstrating love, compassion, forgiveness, and service, we become living examples of Christ's love, subtly yet powerfully inspiring those around us to follow Him. Our actions are our most compelling sermons, our lives are the most potent testimonies, and our consistent faith is the strongest invitation to join us in experiencing the transformative power of God's grace.

This process of inspiring others through our lives is not a passive endeavor; it is a continuous journey of growth and refinement. It requires conscious effort, consistent prayer, and a willingness to allow God to work through us. It is a commitment to self-reflection, recognizing areas where we can improve, and striving to live more fully in accordance with God's will. It's a journey of continuous learning and growth, both personally and spiritually.

Finally, remember that we are not alone in this journey. We have the support of the Spirit of God, the guidance of Scripture, and the fellowship of our Christian community. Lean on these resources, seek out mentors and accountability partners, and never underestimate the power of prayer. As you strive to live a life that inspires others, you will find that you are also being deeply blessed and transformed by God's grace. Your legacy, then, becomes not just your own, but a tapestry woven from threads of faith, hope, and love, a testament to the transformative power of God's grace in the lives of women who courageously embrace their calling to inspire others. The ripples you create will extend beyond your lifetime, a lasting legacy of faith that will continue to touch and transform lives for generations to come.

**Your ministry is found where you've been broken—your testimony is found where you've been restored.**

Sharing your testimony is not about boasting; it's about bearing witness. It's about offering a glimpse into the transformative power of God's grace in your own life, a beacon of hope for others navigating their own journeys of faith. Think of it as passing the torch, sharing the light you've received so others may find their way. Your story, unique and deeply personal, holds the potential to ignite a spark of faith in another's heart, offering solace, encouragement, and a tangible reminder of God's unwavering love.

The power of a personal testimony lies in its authenticity. It's the raw, unfiltered narrative of your relationship with God, encompassing both the triumphs and the trials, the moments of profound joy and the depths of despair. It's in the honesty of your vulnerability that others find connection, recognizing their own struggles mirrored in your story. It's not about presenting a polished, perfect image; it's about showcasing the genuine, messy, and beautiful reality of faith lived out in the everyday.

Consider the details that make your story unique. Perhaps it's the moment you felt God's presence most powerfully, a turning point in your life that irrevocably altered your trajectory. It might be a time of profound loss or adversity, where you experienced God's unwavering support and comfort, a testament to His faithfulness even in the darkest of hours. It could be a gradual unfolding, a slow but steady revelation of God's presence in the mundane, the ordinary moments where His grace quietly illuminated your path.

Remember the details. What were you feeling? What were you thinking? What sensory details can you recall that bring the moment alive—the smell of rain on the earth, the warmth of the sun on your skin, the sound of a loved one's voice offering comfort? These seemingly insignificant details hold the power to connect with others on a deeply emotional level, creating a powerful narrative that resonates long after the words have been spoken.

Don't shy away from the challenging parts of your story. The struggles, the doubts, the moments when your faith wavered—these are not imperfections; they are integral parts of your journey. These moments demonstrate that faith isn't about unwavering certainty; it's about unwavering commitment, even amidst the uncertainty. Your vulnerability invites others to share their own struggles without shame or fear of judgment. It creates a space of empathy, understanding, and shared experience, fostering a sense of community and mutual support.

Structuring your testimony can be simple. You could begin with a brief introduction, setting the stage for your story. Then, narrate the pivotal events, focusing on the specific moments when God's presence was particularly evident. Weave in scriptural references that resonate with your experience, showing how God's word provided comfort, guidance, or understanding. Conclude by sharing the lessons you learned and how your relationship with God has been transformed. Remember, the goal isn't to create a flawless narrative; it's to convey the essence of your experience with God's grace and faithfulness.

Practice sharing your testimony with trusted friends or family members first. This allows you to refine your story, become more comfortable sharing it, and receive helpful feedback. Seek out a safe and supportive environment where you feel comfortable expressing your vulnerabilities and sharing the intimate details of your journey with God. Their encouragement and affirmation will build your confidence and help you to refine your storytelling.

Consider different venues for sharing your testimony. It could be within your church community, during a small group meeting, or at a women's retreat. You could also share your testimony with friends and family members during informal gatherings or even through writing—a blog post, a journal entry, or a personal letter. The key is to find the appropriate setting and audience for your message, one where your words will resonate and inspire others and continue to help you heal.

Your testimony isn't just a story; it's an act of service. It's a way of offering hope to those who feel lost, encouragement to those who are struggling, and a testament to the transformative power of God's grace. In sharing your experience, you become a living example of God's love, demonstrating His faithfulness and reminding others that they are not alone in their journey. Remember, your story holds the potential to make a profound impact, not only on those who hear it directly but also on those whose lives are touched through the ripple effect of your testimony.

Think of the women in Scripture whose lives have inspired countless others. Their stories, etched into the pages of the Bible, are testaments to God's unwavering faithfulness and their courageous response to His calling. Deborah, a judge and prophetess, led her people to victory; Esther, a queen, risked her life to save her people; Ruth, a loyal Moabite woman, demonstrated unwavering faithfulness to her mother-in-law; Hannah, a barren woman, persisted in prayer, receiving a miraculous answer. These women, despite facing immense challenges, remained steadfast in their faith, leaving a powerful legacy that continues to inspire women today. Their stories are powerful examples of how faith, courage, and perseverance can transform lives and leave a lasting legacy. Their lives demonstrate that sharing our personal testimonies is not simply an option; it is a sacred responsibility.

While we often read about these remarkable women in the Bible, it's crucial to recognize that they were, above all, ordinary individuals navigating their everyday lives within the context of their time—much like you and I do today. They couldn't have imagined that their stories would be immortalized and shared across generations. Nor could they foresee that Karen Pless Gaines would draw upon their experiences in this book, to inspire countless others. Their lives remind us that each of us has the potential to impact those around us, even when we least expect it.

The act of sharing your testimony is itself an act of faith, a testament to your belief in the power of God's grace to transform lives. It requires courage, vulnerability, and a willingness to be open and honest about your own journey. But the rewards are immeasurable. In sharing your story, you not only inspire others but also deepen your own faith, reaffirming your relationship with God and solidifying your commitment to His calling. It is a reciprocal act, one that strengthens your faith as you share it with others.

The impact of your testimony may not be immediately apparent. It may be a small seed planted in a heart, nurtured over time, eventually blossoming into a vibrant faith. It may be a word of comfort offered during a time of despair, a light of hope illuminating a dark path. Or it might be a catalyst for transformation, inspiring someone to seek a deeper relationship with God. Whatever the outcome, your testimony serves as a powerful testament to God's grace, a beacon of hope, and a legacy of faith that will continue to inspire others for generations to come.

Your life, with its triumphs and struggles, is a living testament to God's faithfulness. Sharing your testimony is not an optional extra; it is a vital part of your calling as a Christian woman. It is an opportunity to inspire others, to share the hope and encouragement you've received, and to make a lasting impact on the world around you. Embrace this opportunity to bear witness to God's incredible grace in your life, and let your testimony be a source of hope and encouragement for others on their journey of faith. Remember, your story matters. It's a unique tapestry woven with threads of faith, perseverance, and God's unwavering love—a story that deserves to be shared.

**What you leave behind will help someone move mountains.**

The journey of faith, much like life itself, is not a destination but a continuous unfolding. We are constantly evolving, growing, learning, and deepening our relationship with God. The lessons learned, the challenges overcome, and the triumphs celebrated along the way shape us, molding us into the women God intended us to be. This process of spiritual maturation is not a sprint; it's a marathon, requiring patience, perseverance, and unwavering faith.

Think of the biblical accounts of women like Ruth. Her unwavering loyalty to Naomi, her commitment to God's principles, and her willingness to embrace the unknown, ultimately led her to Boaz and a life beyond what she could have imagined. Her story isn't just a romantic tale, but a testament to the ongoing journey of faith, a constant unfolding of God's plan. Ruth's commitment didn't end with her marriage; her faith continued to shape her life, demonstrating the continuous nature of spiritual growth. We see this same principle throughout Scripture. The women of faith were not static figures, they continued to grow and evolve in their faith, responding to God's guidance and adapting to changing circumstances.

This continuous journey necessitates a commitment to ongoing learning. This isn't solely about formal theological studies, although those can be enriching. It's about actively engaging with God's Word, seeking His wisdom through prayer and meditation, and allowing the Holy Ghost to guide and direct your steps. Consider joining a Bible study group, engaging in spiritual mentorship, or seeking out resources that enrich your understanding of scripture and deepen your faith. These practices are not optional extras; they are essential components of a thriving spiritual life. They provide nourishment and support for the continuous growth of our faith. Regularly engaging with God's Word allows us to

223

discover new layers of meaning, receive fresh insights, and gain a deeper understanding of His love and grace.

Moreover, the spiritual journey is inherently relational. It's not a solitary pursuit but a path traveled in community with other believers. Surrounding yourself with supportive, faith-filled women is crucial for navigating the challenges and celebrating the triumphs of life. These women can provide accountability, encouragement, and a safe space for sharing your vulnerabilities and seeking guidance. A strong support system is vital for spiritual growth, providing comfort during difficult times and inspiration during moments of doubt.

This network of faith-filled relationships is not just limited to fellow believers. It extends to our families, our friends, and even strangers we encounter along the way. Consider how we can share our faith, our hope, and our love with those around us, not in a judgmental or **proselytizing** manner, but through acts of kindness, compassion, and genuine care. Our actions should reflect our beliefs. Sharing our faith is an integral part of our spiritual journey, a way to demonstrate the transformative power of God's love. In sharing our faith, we often find that we are also the recipients of blessings, unexpected sources of comfort, and support from those around us. The continuous journey is often a reciprocal one.

Another critical aspect of our ongoing spiritual journey is the cultivation of self-awareness. This involves taking time for introspection, examining our hearts, and seeking to align our thoughts, feelings, and actions with God's will. This process of self-reflection can be uncomfortable, requiring us to confront our weaknesses, acknowledge our flaws, and repent for our shortcomings. But it is through this process of honest self-assessment that we grow spiritually, shedding old patterns of behavior and embracing new ones that are aligned with God's purpose. Remember the parable of the talents; we are all given unique gifts and abilities; the continuous journey of faith requires us to identify and develop those talents. It requires introspection to understand what our abilities are and to put them to use for God's glory.

Do you remember the lady from California I mentioned earlier? Her insights made a significant impact on my life. That night, I found myself deep in conversation with God, grappling with the revelations she shared. Initially, I was defensive, thinking, "God, I don't do that; why would she say such a thing?" I even questioned, "How could she possibly know me?" But I chose to open my heart and let God guide me in reflecting on these matters.

Her words compelled me to think critically and ask the hard questions. Through His incredible grace, God helped me recognize the areas in my life that needed change and the burdens I needed to release. So, please don't shy away from seeking help when it comes to identifying what needs improvement in your life. Likewise, don't hesitate to share your insights with others; your honesty could be the very catalyst someone else needs for transformation. Remember, your obedience can empower others to move mountains in their own lives.

Remember that the journey also includes embracing our strengths and celebrating our accomplishments. It's easy to get caught up in self-doubt, minimizing our achievements and focusing on our shortcomings. But God calls us to embrace our strengths, to recognize the gifts He has bestowed upon us, and to use those gifts for His glory. This is a part of recognizing the legacy of faith that we are building, recognizing the positive impact that our lives can have on those around us. Celebrating our accomplishments, both big and small, allows us to acknowledge God's hand in our lives and strengthens our faith in His plan for us. The continuous journey is not just about growth but also about the acknowledgment of the successes along the way.

Continuing our spiritual journey means embracing the challenges and difficulties life throws our way. These challenges are not obstacles meant to deter us but opportunities for growth and refinement. Through perseverance, we learn to trust God's plan, even amidst uncertainty and pain. These challenges refine our faith, build our resilience, and deepen our dependence on God. We find our strength renewed, not by avoiding difficulties, but by facing them with faith and courage.

Our spiritual growth doesn't stop; it's an ongoing process of refinement and transformation. We must be willing to adapt and change as we encounter new circumstances and experiences. This is not a sign of weakness but of spiritual maturity. Our faith must be flexible and dynamic, allowing us to evolve and grow alongside our changing lives. This constant evolution is part of our legacy of faith. We are called to be adaptable, to embrace the changing times, and to continue learning and evolving in our faith.

As we continue on our spiritual journey, it's essential to remember that we are not alone. God is always with us, providing guidance, comfort, and strength. He walks alongside us, offering unwavering support, even when we stumble or falter. His love is constant, His grace is sufficient, and His presence is our unwavering companion on this lifelong journey. Remembering this enduring presence of God provides comfort, encouragement, and strength during the difficult moments. It allows us to keep moving forward, trusting in His plan, even when we can't see the path ahead.

Finally, let us never underestimate the power of prayer. Prayer is not merely a ritual; it's a lifeline to God, a way of connecting with Him, sharing our joys and sorrows, seeking His guidance, and receiving His comfort. Through prayer, we deepen our relationship with God, allowing Him to shape and mold us into the women He has called us to be. Prayer provides the daily nourishment and guidance required for continued spiritual growth. It provides a sense of connection with the divine, a feeling of support that is essential to our ongoing journey.

The journey of faith is a lifelong commitment, a constant process of growth, learning, and refinement. It's a journey of embracing both the triumphs and the trials, celebrating the blessings, and persevering through the challenges. It's a journey of continually deepening our relationship with God, sharing our faith with others, and leaving a legacy of love and devotion. Embracing this continuous journey allows us to become the best versions of ourselves, fulfilling God's purpose for our lives and leaving a lasting impact on the world around us. Remember, the path is ongoing; the journey continues; and God's grace is sufficient for every step of the way. The ultimate legacy is not merely the accomplishments we achieve, but the faith we share, the love we give, and the lives we touch along the way. So, rise with Grace and let the warrior spirit awaken in you.

## Discussion Questions

1. What are some everyday choices you can make to positively impact those around you?

2. Who are the women in your life that have inspired you, and what specific qualities do you admire in them?

3. How can living out your faith in daily interactions create a lasting legacy?

4. What does integrity mean to you, and how do you practice it in your everyday life?

5. In what small ways can you demonstrate kindness and generosity to others?

6. How has mentorship played a role in your life, and how can you become a mentor for someone else?

7. What community initiatives or causes resonate with you, and how can you contribute to them?

8. How do you nurture your relationships with family and friends to build a strong legacy of love and connection?

9. What form of written expression (journals, letters, family history) do you feel would best convey your values and experiences for future generations?

10. In what ways can you remind yourself that leaving a positive legacy is an ongoing journey and not a destination?

# Acknowledgments

First and foremost, I offer heartfelt thanks to God, the source of all strength and inspiration. This book would not exist without His unwavering guidance and grace. To my family, particularly my husband and children, thank you for your patience, understanding, and unwavering support throughout the writing process. Your love has been my constant anchor. A special thank you to my dear friends and mentors, Kiara Espinoza, Brandie Fowler, and Hannah Espinoza, whose encouragement and late-night talks have been invaluable. You women have been a pillar of strength, and your shared stories and experiences have immeasurably enriched this work. Finally, I express my deepest gratitude to my Lord and Savior, Jesus Christ. Without Him, this book would never have come into existence.

# GLOSSARY

**Proselytizing-** The action of attempting to convert someone from one religion, belief, or opinion to another.

# CITED

https://www.biblegateway.com/

This book contains information based on my life experiences and Bible study. The scripture references used in this book are drawn primarily from the Specify Bible translation, e.g., New International Version (NIV), English Standard Version (ESV), and King James Version (KJV).

# ABOUT THE AUTHOR

Karen Pless Gaines is a Christian author, inspirational speaker, and women's ministry leader. She has dedicated her life to empowering women to discover and fulfill their God-given potential. With years of experience in biblical studies, she combines a deep understanding of biblical principles with practical, real-world applications. Karen is passionate about equipping women to navigate the challenges of life with faith, grace, and unwavering strength. She is the author of Breaking the Silence: Generational Curse Breakers, Woman of Valor: conquering Toxic People God's Way, and many others. You can connect with her on Facebook-- @authorkpgaines .